I0235379

IMAGES
of America

VENTURA COUNTY

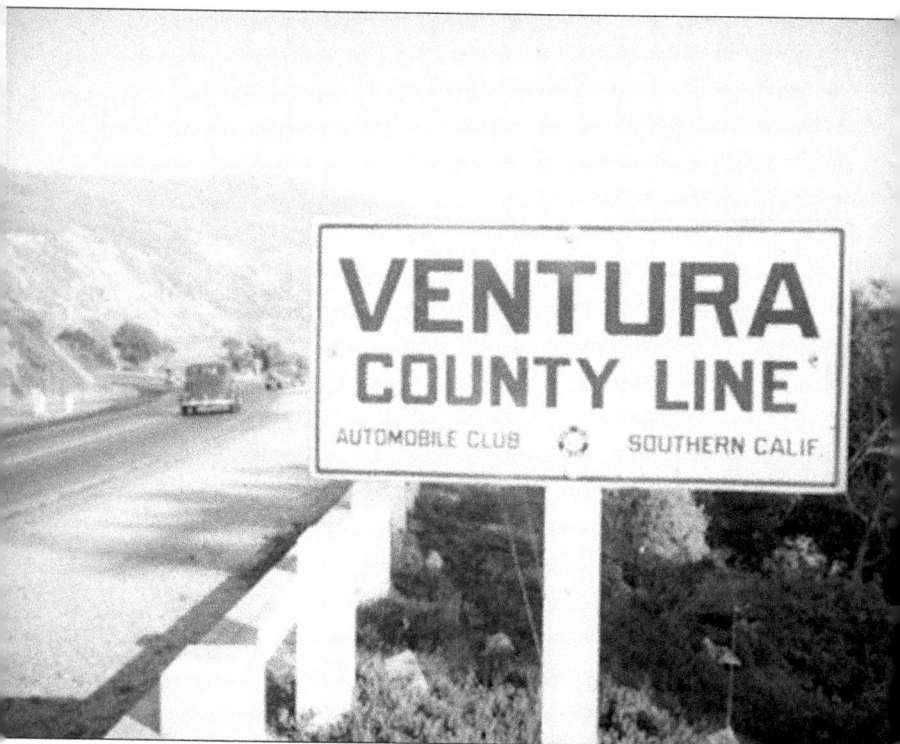

Seen here in 1937 is a county line sign posted by the Automobile Club of Southern California around 1916. The Ventura branch of the auto club opened in 1917, the 10th branch since the club's founding in 1900. Ten years before the Ventura branch opened, the auto club installed the first directional signs along Ventura County's roads. (Courtesy of John Randolph and Dora Haynes Foundation.)

ON THE COVER: An orange-picking crew poses in Fillmore in 1893. Picking oranges was labor intensive before mechanical harvesting was developed. Crews were needed to pick the oranges and crate them in the orchards. (Courtesy of Fillmore Historical Museum.)

IMAGES
of America

VENTURA COUNTY

Carina Monica Montoya

ARCADIA
PUBLISHING

Copyright © 2021 by Carina Monica Montoya
ISBN 978-1-5402-4781-0

Published by Arcadia Publishing
Charleston, South Carolina

Library of Congress Control Number: 2021936563

For all general information, please contact Arcadia Publishing:
Telephone 843-853-2070
Fax 843-853-0044
E-mail sales@arcadiapublishing.com
For customer service and orders:
Toll-Free 1-888-313-2665

Visit us on the Internet at www.arcadiapublishing.com

This book is dedicated to the people of Ventura County who embrace its history, beauty, and diversity. More importantly, to those who have been diligent in keeping safe and supporting others and local businesses during COVID-19 isolation and the ensuing trying times.

CONTENTS

FOREWORD

Ventura County is a marvelous mixture of history, industry, agriculture, and community. The rich alluvial soil has yielded abundant crops that have fed the region and the nation for generations. Its cities and towns, from Simi to Piru to Ventura and Ojai, are unique, attractive, and welcoming.

The land is littered with place names whose origins span millennia. The descendants of those who first bestowed these names—Topatopa, Sespe, and Hueneme—are still here, residing in the valleys and canyons and along the shoreline where their ancestors hunted and fished, worked and worshipped, and lived and died.

Later arrivals left their imprints in the form of a mission, adobes, oil wells, a railroad, highways, towns, schools, libraries, farms, and factories. It is an important location for the US military, with Naval Air Station Point Mugu, Naval Construction Battalion Center Point Hueneme, and US Coast Guard Station Channel Islands Harbor.

Carina Forsythe, an accomplished researcher, author, and historian, is a retired veteran, having served in both the US Coast Guard Reserve and the US Navy Reserve. She has given us another fine volume to enjoy marvelous photographs and stories. Read this book and take it with you as you search out your own favorite places. Some of these might include the Los Padres National Forest and the Santa Monica Mountains and seaward to the coast and the Channel Islands.

Take it from world-class climber and businessman Yvon Chouinard, who wrote, "When I moved my shop [Chouinard Equipment Company] to Ventura to be closer to the surf, the ultimate day was what we called a 'McNab'; skiing on Pine Mountain, climbing on the Sespe Wall, playing tennis, and surfing the glass-off at C Street or Rincon. Where else in the world except New Zealand could you pull off a day like that?"

The answer is Ventura County!

Robert C. Pavlik
Historian, Author, and Poet
September 27, 2020

ACKNOWLEDGMENTS

I am most grateful to Martha Gentry, president and executive director of the Fillmore Historical Museum, for her gracious and generous support in opening the museum doors to me at a time when the spread of COVID-19 necessitated the close of nonessential businesses. I am also very grateful to Sue Zeider at the Fillmore Historical Museum, who provided me with a substantial pool of archived photographs and reference materials from which to review and select. Both Martha and Sue have gone above and beyond in giving me their time, trust, and resources to make this book possible.

I am also very grateful to Carol Anderson, curator of history at the Stagecoach Inn Museum, who opened the museum doors to me and was very generous in providing me with photographs, reference materials, and editing.

My deep appreciation goes to Ann Huston, former chief of cultural resources for Channel Islands National Park. Ann provided me with many historical photographs and information on Anacapa Island.

I am indebted to Steven Dale Walker for his time in taking many photographs around the county. I am also indebted to my dear friend Dan Klos for his IT service in the preparation of the photographs. Much appreciation to my best friend Dennis Bougher for his support in all my endeavors. Many thanks to John Noble and others who helped me gather resources.

It has been an honor that my friend Robert C. Pavlik, a retired environmental planner, historian, and author, has provided me with ongoing professional assistance, guidance, and pre-submission reviews on my books, including this one on Ventura County, a place that is very personal and dear to him.

INTRODUCTION

Ventura County lies between Los Angeles and Santa Barbara Counties, with Kern County on the north. It has one of the most varied and picturesque natural landscapes of ocean, mountains, valleys, unique rock formations, rivers, creeks, hot springs, and forests. For thousands of years, Chumash Indians inhabited the coastal lands and Channel Islands until the Spanish Portolá expedition in 1769 arrived on the Pacific coast. Junípero Serra, a Franciscan priest from Spain, voyaged with other clergy on the expedition to the New World as missionaries to spread Christianity. To that end, 21 missions were built along California's coastal region from San Diego to Sonoma. The missions were built along El Camino Real (the Royal Highway), with each mission about a day's journey from the next. Ventura became the locus for the San Buenaventura Mission. It was intended to be the third mission in California, but its construction was delayed until 1782, at which time it became the ninth mission in the chain and the last mission Junipero Serra founded before his death in 1784.

After Mexico's independence from Spain in 1821, missions became secularized and their expansive lands became the property of the Mexican government. Mission lands were divided into large ranchos and granted to individuals with political influence and to former soldiers for their service during the war.

The Mexican-American War (1846–1848) ended with the signing of the Treaty of Guadalupe Hidalgo in February 1848. Under the treaty, the United States paid Mexico $15 million for the purchase of California. Gold was soon discovered near Sacramento, which led to the historic California gold rush of 1848, resulting in a population boom in California and a fast-growing need for civil government. In 1849, Californians sought statehood and one year later, California became the 31st state in the union. That same year, California designated its first 27 counties, which included Santa Barbara. In 1873, Santa Barbara County's southern portion was split to create Ventura County and the city of Ventura was made the county seat. San Buenaventura is the oldest city in the county and was incorporated in 1866 while it was still part of Santa Barbara County.

Rancho Ojai was settled in the 1800s and was primarily used for cattle ranching. In 1864, it was sold to Pennsylvania railroad and oil baron Thomas A. Scott, whose nephew Thomas Bard discovered oil on the north side of Sulphur Mountain. In 1890, Union Oil Company of California was founded with Bard as president. It was headquartered in Santa Paula.

Meiners Oaks, a small community west of Ojai, was named after John Meiners, who purchased the land in the 1870s and farmed citrus, plums, apricots, apples, and grains. Nearby Matilija Hot Springs was discovered in 1873 by J.W. Wilcox, who purchased the springs for therapeutic bathing. The springs were sold in 1875 to R.M. Brown, who opened them to the public in 1877. Nearby Wheeler Springs was founded in 1891 by Wheeler Blumberg, who built a small resort.

El Rio is a small community founded in 1875 and originally named New Jerusalem after a store owned by Jewish immigrant Simon Cohn (1852–1936). The town's name was changed to El Rio in 1895. A post office was established in 1882, and three years later a one-room schoolhouse opened as well as Santa Clara Catholic Church. The church was the second Catholic church founded in the county since Mission San Buenaventura. In 1837, Rancho Calleguas was settled by Jose Pedro Ruiz, who later sold the land to Juan Camarillo. Juan's sons Adolfo and Juan Jr. are credited as the founders of the town of Camarillo.

Casitas Springs was first recorded under the name Arroyo de Las Casitas in 1864. It was one of the county's oldest small towns. In 1878, a stagecoach road was constructed over the Casitas Pass. Nearby Oak View was established in the late 1940s and is a small community along the Ventura River nestled in a narrow valley between Casitas Springs and Mira Monte. From 1898 to 1969, the Ventura & Ojai Valley Railroad served the small rural community of Mira Monte. The railroad enabled Ojai to connect with the national rail network.

Saticoy was part of Rancho Santa Paula y Saticoy, granted to Manuel Jimeno Casarin in 1840. In 1861, Jefferson L. Crane was one of the first American settlers in the area, but in 1868 W.D.F. Richards purchased 650 acres for farming and was instrumental in developing the town. Cabrillo Village was once a labor camp. The Saticoy Lemon Growers Association built and designated the area in 1936 to house its farm workers. Seventy-six years later, farmworkers who were threatened with eviction joined together and purchased the village. It became an affordable housing cooperative with resident ownership and control.

Also part of the former Rancho Santa Paula y Saticoy is Santa Paula. The town was laid out in 1872 when Nathan Weston Blanchard purchased land and soon began planting orange trees. The area is designated as part of Ventura County's Santa Paula–Fillmore Greenbelt.

Thomas Bard founded the town of Point Hueneme in 1874. He had the Hueneme Wharf constructed in 1871, which became the main hub of transportation for that area. It was the second-largest grain shipping port on the coast from 1871 to 1895.

Fillmore was founded in 1887 when a rail line was built through the Santa Clara River Valley. The town was named after J.A. Fillmore, general superintendent of the railroad's Pacific division. When the railroad reached the Santa Clara River Valley, the towns of Santa Paula, Fillmore, and Piru began to grow, along with the citrus industry. The small community of Bardsdale just outside of Fillmore was established in 1887 by Royce G. Surdam (1835–1891). In the early years, barley, cabbage, and potatoes were grown there. In later years, the area became known for its orange, lemon, and avocado orchards.

In 1888, David C. Cook laid out the town of Piru and built a rail line to service the town. In 1890, Cook built a Queen Anne Victorian mansion that was destroyed by fire in 1981 but rebuilt by its new owner.

Rancho Camulos was part of Rancho San Francisco, granted to Antonio del Valle. After his death in 1841, his son Ygnacio del Valle inherited the rancho and used the land for livestock ranching and agriculture, but its primary product was wine. It is recorded that the ranch was the largest vintner in the area.

The Conejo Valley was part of the 1803 Mexican land grant Rancho El Conejo granted to Ignacio Rodriguez and José Polanco for grazing or use rights, not ownership. In 1822, Polanco abandoned his rights, and his half of the rancho was granted to José de la Guerra. In 1872, de la Guerra sold his half of the rancho to John Edwards and Howard W. Mills, who acquired most of the original rancho lands, selling smaller portions to Egbert Starr Newbury and C.E. Huse. Newbury purchased 2,259 acres of the rancho that spanned from Old Town Thousand Oaks to present-day Newbury Park. In 1875, Newbury established the Conejo Valley's first post office, and the Conejo Valley School District was established in 1877. Newbury Park was on a stagecoach route between Santa Barbara and Los Angeles. The Grand Union Hotel, later the Conejo Hotel and the Stagecoach Inn, offered lodging for travelers.

In 1881, Mills sold Triunfo Ranch, now Westlake Village, to Andrew Russell. Later, the Westlake tract was divided at the Ventura/Los Angeles County line and two sections of the Westlake development on the Ventura County side were annexed into the City of Thousand Oaks in 1968 and 1972. Located in the Santa Monica Mountains, Lake Sherwood reservoir was built in 1901 with the small community of Lake Sherwood overlooking it. One of the main attractions in Thousand Oaks from the mid-1920s to the late 1960s was Jungleland USA, an animal-themed park. It first opened in 1925 as Goebel's Lion Farm. In 1929, it was renamed Goebel's Wild Animal Farm. In 1946, the park was sold and renamed World Jungle Compound. It was sold again in 1956 and renamed Jungleland USA, and closed for good in 1969.

Thousand Oaks became the first city to incorporate in the Conejo Valley and the second most populous city in Ventura County. Simi Valley was once Rancho San José de Nuestra Señora de Altagracia y Simi, also called Rancho Simi. It was one of the largest land grants in Alta California. The land was granted to Santiago Pico in 1795 and then re-granted to Santiago's three sons after his death in 1815. In 1842, Capt. José de la Guerra y Noriega of the Santa Barbara Presidio purchased Rancho Simi from the Pico brothers. After de la Guerra's death in 1858, his sons continued to work the ranchos until the family lost ownership of both El Rancho Simi in 1865 and El Rancho Tapo in the 1880s. Although El Rancho Tapo was part of El Rancho Simi, it was treated as a separate rancho. The first American pioneer who purchased El Rancho Simi was Thomas A. Scott. Thomas Bard managed Scott's California properties. In the late 1880s, the Simi Land and Water Company was founded. The company divided the lands into smaller properties and sold them as ranches and farms.

Simi Valley has four distinct communities: Simi, Santa Susana, Community Center, and Mortimer Park. Simi's first neighborhood was established when colony houses, which consisted of a dozen pre-cut and partially assembled houses from Chicago, were brought to Simi. The town of Santa Susana came into existence when the train depot was built in 1903. Soon, a business center began to grow near the depot and residential development followed. Residential growth began in the 1920s, and shortly thereafter the area's first high school, elementary school, and Methodist church were founded. The Santa Susana Knolls area was originally called Mortimer Park and comprised 1,800 acres of land purchased by T. Lewis Mortimer and his wife in the 1920s for the purpose of selling the land in lots for cabins and houses. In 1944, the name was changed to Santa Susana Knolls.

Simi Valley was home to some of the country's pioneering development of nuclear reactors, rocket engines, and energy technology engineering. It is also home to the Ronald Reagan Presidential Library, the largest of the country's 13 presidential libraries.

Moorpark was founded in 1900 when approval for the Moorpark Post Office was granted. The area was also once part of Rancho Simi. The 1904 completion of a 7,369-foot tunnel through the Santa Susana Mountains put Moorpark on the Southern Pacific Railroad Coast Line route between San Francisco and Los Angeles.

In 1898, the town of Oxnard was founded by Henry T. Oxnard, who constructed a sugar beet factory there. The factory became such a large industry and employer that a rail line was built to serve it. The industry brought many people to live and work in Oxnard, and the land attracted livestock ranchers and farmers. The town was incorporated as the City of Oxnard on June 30, 1903, and its fast growth made it the largest city in the county.

Port Hueneme got its start in 1870 when W.E. Barnard settled with others in Rancho El Rio de Santa Clara o La Colonia. Later, naval bases Point Mugu and Port Hueneme came around World War II. It was an ideal coastal military location between San Francisco Bay and the Port of Los Angeles.

From Spanish colonization of Alta California and its missions to Mexican California and its ranchos, and from early American expansion to the present day, its history is what makes Ventura County unique. The county's communities, businesses, and workforce reflect its diversity. Despite being hit by catastrophic events and disasters through the years, including the COVID-19 pandemic, the people of Ventura County have always picked up the pieces, rebuilt, and continued to live in a place they call home.

One

ANACAPA AND
SAN NICOLAS ISLANDS

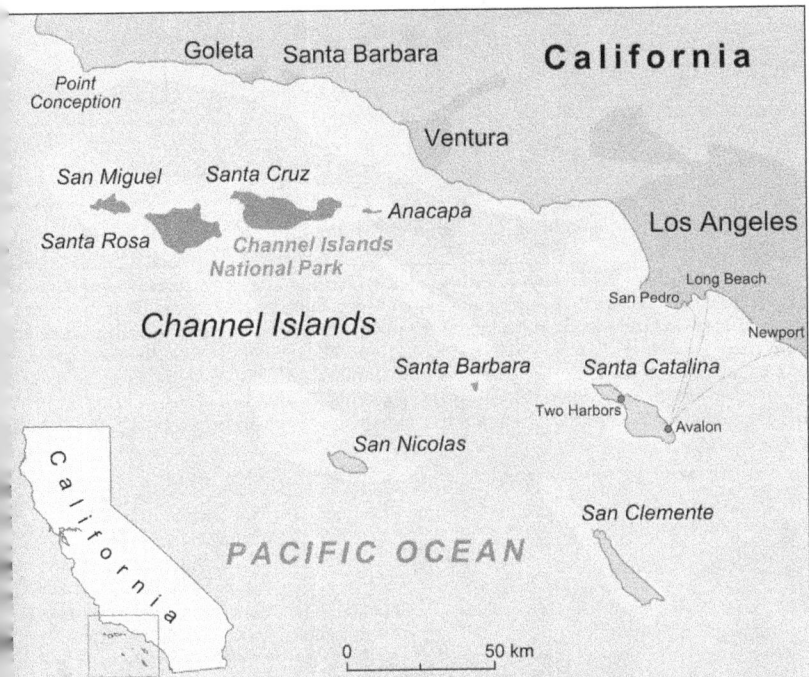

The Channel Islands is an archipelago of eight islands that span 160 miles along the coast of Los Angeles, Ventura, and Santa Barbara Counties. Anacapa and San Nicolas Islands are within Ventura County. Archaeological and ethnographic studies indicate that native peoples occupied San Nicolas Island as far back as 8,000 years ago. Chumash people had encampments on Anacapa Island more than 5,000 years ago. (Image by Lencer, Wikimedia Commons.)

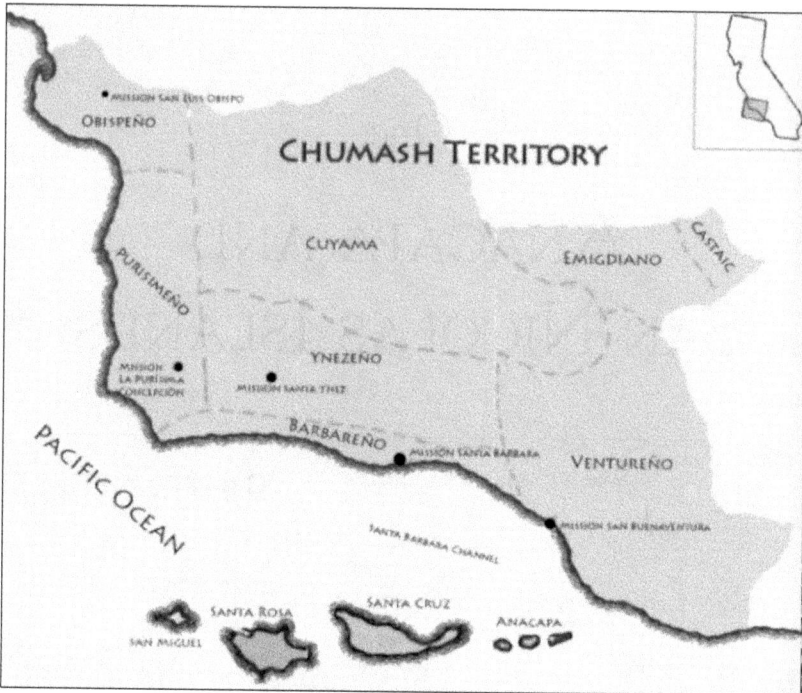

Pictured is a map showing Chumash territory that primarily spanned California's south-central coast from Malibu Canyon in Los Angeles County to San Luis Obispo in Santa Barbara County, Santa Barbara Channel Islands, and inland to the western end of the San Joaquin Valley. Chumash is the name for several California Indian groups who spoke similar languages. Some groups were later named after the missions they were associated with, such as Obispeño from Mission San Luis Obispo, Purisimeño from Mission La Purisima Conception, Barbareño for Mission Santa Barbara, and Ventureño for Mission San Buenaventura. (Courtesy of Damian Bacich.)

This is a painting of a Chumash *tomol*. The Chumash were a maritime culture, and they constructed these water vessels resembling a long canoe to navigate around the Channel Islands. The tomol was constructed of pine planks or redwood and sealed with a melted and boiled mixture of hard tar and pine pitch. (Courtesy of Stagecoach Inn Museum.)

Seen here is an 1877 photograph of a Chumash chief of the Ineseño Chumash community of Zanja de Cota. He is also sometimes referred to as a medicine man. His Chumash name was Samala, but it was later changed to Rafael Solares. Solares posed for this photograph wearing traditional dancing regalia in the Santa Ynez area. He was likely associated with Mission Santa Inés in neighboring Santa Barbara County. (Courtesy of Stagecoach Inn Museum.)

This is an early 1900s photograph of Candelaria Valenzuela, a Chumash Ventureño basket weaver. There were three distinct Chumash languages: Obispeño, Ysleño or Cruzeño, and Central Chumash. The different languages were characteristic of each region, such as the northern portion of the coast, Channel Islands, and the Central Coast. The Central Chumash had four dialects: Barbareño, Inseño, Purisimeño, and Ventureño. Ventureño was spoken from the Ventura area to Simi Hills and south to Malibu. (Courtesy of Black Gold Cooperative Library System.)

13

The Chumash lived and thrived in their settlements on the coastal mainland and islands. Pictured are two young Chumash males playing a popular game of throwing a long pole or stick through a rolling hoop made of branches or bark. It helped the young to develop skills for hunting and crafts. In the background are *aps*, structures where families lived. Aps were typically round and made of grass and reeds fastened to long poles. (Courtesy of Stagecoach Inn Museum.)

A reconstructed traditional ap is seen here. Aps were dome-shaped and covered with layers of local bulrush and animal skins when it rained. An open hole at the top served as a vent and allowed for air circulation. The structure was often made of redwood, cedar, or whalebone and was sturdy. Aps were typically 12 to 20 feet in diameter. (Courtesy of Stagecoach Inn Museum.)

This aerial photograph of Anacapa Island was taken in 2009. Located approximately 14 miles from the Ventura harbor, it was formed by volcanic activity several million years ago, and its composition is a mixture of lava, breccias, volcanic ash, and cinders. Erosion and years of waves affected the lava formation and caused the island to separate into islets. The three islets are called East, Middle, and West Anacapa. (Courtesy of National Park Service.)

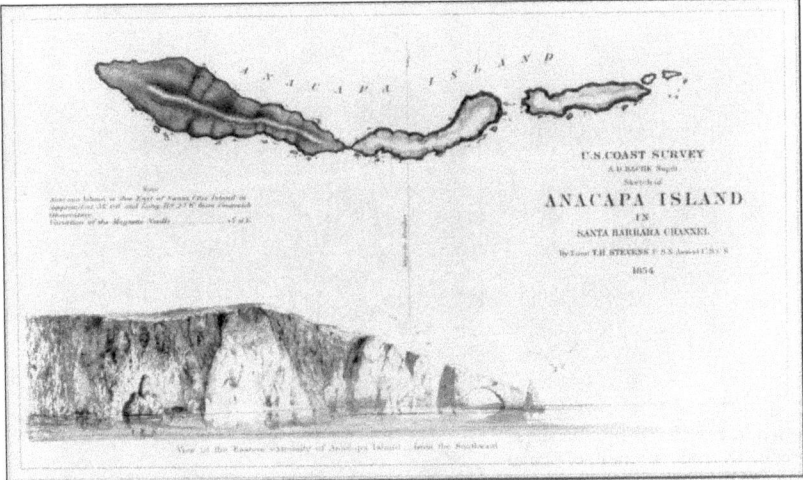

This is a sketch from an 1854 US Coast Survey map of Anacapa Island illustrating a view of the eastern extremity of the island from the south. Measuring about five miles long and a half-mile wide, it is one of the smallest of the Channel Islands. The map was created by James Abbott McNeill Whistler (1834–1903), regarded as one of the most influential figures of the 19th-century art world. (Courtesy of Library of Congress.)

Pictured are the boat hoist and boathouse on East Anacapa at Landing Cove in 1931. Small boats were lifted out of the water onto land. Shipments of materials and resources were delivered to the landing dock. (Photograph by Fred S. Cobb, courtesy of Channel Islands National Park.)

A tender lies offshore of Anacapa Island in 1932. Large boats or ships required a tender to transport cargo and people to the island. Tenders were once used to service other boats and ships that were unable to dock at the island. (Photograph by Fred S. Cobb, courtesy of Channel Islands National Park.)

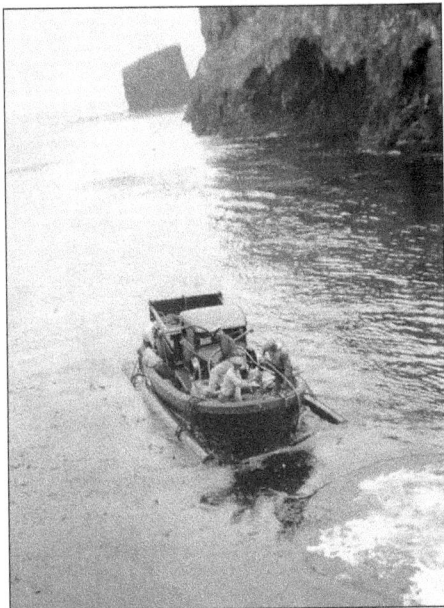

In this 1932 photograph, a tender transports a pickup truck to Anacapa Island. Aboard the tender is Fred S. Cobb (wearing a military-style hat) and four assistants. Cobb was Anacapa's head lighthouse keeper from 1933 to 1935. (Photograph by Fred S. Cobb, courtesy of Channel Islands National Park.)

Pictured in this 1932 photograph is Anacapa's boat hoist in action. Everything that came ashore to the island entered at the eastern end either by climbing the steps up the steep and rugged rock cliff or being hauled up by the hoist. (Photograph by Fred S. Cobb, courtesy of Channel Islands National Park.)

17

An assistant holds on to cables as Fred Cobb, at the stern, looks over the side of a small boat being hoisted up from the landing cove in 1932. Hoisting up the rugged rock cliff was done very carefully. (Photograph by Fred S. Cobb, courtesy of Channel Islands National Park.)

Pictured are US Coast Guard dwellings on East Anacapa in 1932. Early residents of East Anacapa in 1907 were Heaman Bayfield Webster, his wife, and two sons. Another early resident who came to the island in 1928 was Raymond "Frenchy" LeDreau, who occupied several cabins on West Anacapa. LeDreau later became an unofficial caretaker of the island for the National Park Service until 1956. (Photograph by Fred S. Cobb, courtesy of Channel Islands National Park.)

The Anacapa Island Lighthouse was built in 1932 on the highest point of East Anacapa. Standing at 40 feet tall, its third-order Fresnel lens was one of the world's most advanced lighthouse beacons. The light station had a crew of 15–25 people until the 1960s, when the Coast Guard automated the station and controlled it from the mainland. (Photograph by Fred S. Cobb, courtesy of Channel Islands National Park.)

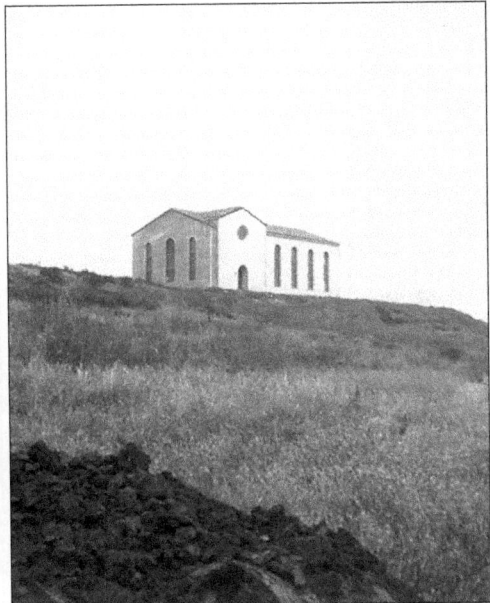

This is a 1932 photograph of Anacapa's tank house, where two 50,000-gallon redwood water tanks were stored. A 30,000 square foot concrete catchment basin was installed behind the structure to funnel rainwater down into the water tanks. The tank house was built by the Coast Guard and resembled a church. The structure preserved water quality and safeguarded the tanks. (Photograph by Fred S. Cobb, courtesy of Channel Islands National Park.)

Seen here is a 1932 photograph of the main road on East Anacapa, on the left. The construction of the light station included the construction of the island's landing dock, a hoisting crane, and roads. After the station was completed, four white stucco houses were built for the lightkeepers and their families. (Photograph by Fred S. Cobb, courtesy of Channel Islands National Park.)

Anacapa Island's flowers are seen here in 1932 with the lighthouse in the background. The island's native vegetation once consisted of alkali heath, buckwheat, California barley, giant ryegrass, goldenbush, gum plant, live-forever, and needlegrass. In the 1940s, the Coast Guard landscaped the island with invasive ice plants for erosion control, which soon engulfed many of the native plants. (Photograph by Fred S. Cobb, courtesy of Channel Islands National Park.)

Located 61 miles off the Ventura County coast, San Nicolas Island is the most remote of the Channel Islands. It was named by Spanish explorer Sebastian Vizcaino after Saint Nicholas in 1602. The island was inhabited for thousands of years by the Chumash Nicoleño tribe, but their population had significantly declined by the early 19th century. (Photograph by Dan from Brussels.)

Juana Maria, better known as the "Lone Woman of San Nicolas Island," lived alone on the island from 1835 to 1853. In 1814, a Russian American Company hunting crew massacred most of the Nicoleño population. In 1835, efforts were made to relocate the remaining Nicoleños to the mainland, except for Juana Maria, who was unintentionally left behind. She was found in 1853 by a hunting crew and brought to the mainland. (Photograph by Edwin J. Hayward and Henry W. Muzzall.)

This is a plaque commemorating Juana Maria and Capt. George Nidever, who brought her to the mainland. Nidever and crew set sail to San Nicolas Island in search of seagull eggs. On the island, they saw footprints in the sand that led them to Juana. This plaque was placed at the Santa Barbara Mission Cemetery in 1928 by the Daughters of the American Revolution. (Author photograph.)

JUANA MARIA
INDIAN WOMAN ABANDONED ON
SAN NICOLAS ISLAND EIGHTEEN YEARS
FOUND AND BROUGHT TO
SANTA BARBARA
BY
CAPT. GEORGE NIDEVER
IN 1853
SANTA BARBARA CHAPTER
DAUGHTERS OF THE
AMERICAN REVOLUTION
1928

Above is a 1574 illustration of men stripping and cutting a whale for its meat and blubber. In 1854, John Davenport established the first shore whaling company in Monterey, California. Davenport sold the company to Portuguese whalers, who dominated the industry until the company closed in 1904. Whales were hunted along the California coast from Crescent City to San Diego. At right, four Japanese crewmen aboard the whaling bark *California* are cutting into a sperm whale, mincing the blubber for trying out. Blubber was heated until the oil separated. It was then cooled, stored in barrels, and sold. Whales were primarily hunted for their blubber and meat. From 1832 to 1937, the steam schooner *California*, along with its two whale catchers *Hawk* and *Port Saunders*, operated off San Nicolas Island and killed approximately 30 finback whales. (Both, courtesy of Library of Congress.)

From 1857 until 1943, the island was used for sheep ranching. The first 500 ewes and some rams came to San Nicolas in 1857, which increased over time to 40,000. The island's vegetation was inadequate to support such large numbers of grazing sheep, and many died of starvation until corrals were constructed for confinement feeding. In the early 1900s, five-year leases were issued to farmers allowing them to live, farm, and graze sheep on the island. (Both, courtesy of Library of Congress.)

Seen here is an aerial view of US Navy facilities on San Nicolas Island. The island is approximately nine miles long and four miles wide and is a naval outlying landing field. Its telemetry equipment supports research, testing, and development across Naval Base Ventura County Point Mugu's 36,000-mile sea range. The Navy gained ownership of San Nicolas Island in 1933. The island was primarily used for patrol aircraft and training. It is integral to the Pacific Missile Range, and in addition to its radar and telemetry facilities, it is also used for missile testing from its several target sites. It is a detachment of Naval Base Ventura County Port Hueneme and Point Mugu. (Courtesy of US Navy.)

Casablanca-class escort carrier USS *Makassar Strait* (CVE-91) was launched in March 1944, commissioned the following month, and decommissioned in August 1946. The ship was named after the Battle of Makassar Strait in World War II. From 1958 to 1960, the former carrier was used as an anchored missile target at San Nicolas Island. It ran aground on the island in 1961 while it was under tow to San Clemente Island in southern California. Below, the *Makassar Strait* is seen breaking up from the impact. She was still used as a target after the wreck. (Both, courtesy of US Navy National Museum of Naval Aviation.)

Two

SAN BUENAVENTURA AND NEIGHBORING TOWNS

This is a late-1700s sketch of Mission San Buenaventura. The history of Ventura County has its roots in the founding of this mission in 1782. The surrounding lands were cultivated for gardens, grain fields, and vineyards, marking the first cultivation of crops in the county. In the 1860s, settlers cultivated lands and began to grow crops commercially as the population grew. Agriculture expansion doubled each decade thereafter, and California became one of the major producers of grain. Ventura County was known as the lima bean capital, utilizing 120,000 acres of land to grow lima beans. (Courtesy of Broome Library, California State University [CSU] Channel Islands.)

Mission San Buenaventura is seen here in the early 1800s. The mission is on East Main and South Figueroa Streets in the city of Ventura. The landmark twin Norfolk pine trees planted in front of the mission in 1880 are not there in this early photograph. The mission church's oldest bells date to 1781. (Courtesy of Broome Library, CSU Channel Islands.)

This is an 1800s photograph of the back side of Mission San Buenaventura. A cluster of connected buildings forming a quadrangle created a compound. The quadrangle included clergy quarters and workshops. The connected buildings were used for crafts such as producing cowhides and tallow, and housed some native mission workers. (Courtesy of Broome Library, CSU Channel Islands.)

This is the interior of Mission San Buenaventura Church in the early 1900s. The first church was destroyed by fire in 1793, and the new church was dedicated in 1809 and reconstructed after an earthquake in 1816. The new church is larger than the earlier one that was destroyed. Constructed of adobe with six-foot-thick walls near the base, the new church was restored in 1893, and again in 1957. (Courtesy of Library of Congress.)

Pictured are the remains of Mission San Buenaventura's aqueduct. The aqueduct was built by the Chumash Indians for the mission between 1805–1815 and was seven miles long and constructed of earth and masonry. It brought water from the San Buenaventura River to the mission. It began at the Compardo Lago and ended at the adobe reservoir behind the mission. (Photograph by Los Angeles, Wikimedia Commons.)

29

Mission San Buenaventura not only began the first cultivation of crops in the county, but also engaged in livestock ranching. By 1816, the mission had over 23,400 cattle, 12,144 sheep, and 4,493 horses. It was the mission with the largest herd of horses. Each mission aimed at becoming self-sufficient. (Courtesy of Library of Congress.)

Each mission planted crops and raised livestock, mainly cattle and sheep. The ranching of livestock and agriculture not only supported the mission community with meat, vegetables, and byproducts such as hides and tallow, but its economy was enhanced by trading its products and crops. Ventura's wide-open lands were ideal for livestock grazing. (Courtesy of Library of Congress.)

Above is a late-1880s photograph of early grain farming. An eight-mule team was used to pull and haul heavy loads and equipment. Mules were a great asset to early farmers. A mule is stronger than a horse of similar size, requires less food than a horse of similar size, and can carry or haul up to 20 percent of its body weight. Below, an 1890s photograph shows a large team of horses pulling a threshing machine. Threshing machines separate wheat, peas, and other small grains and seed crops from their chaff and straw. Early threshing machines were horse- or mule-powered. (Both, courtesy of Broome Library, CSU Channel Islands.)

Main Street in downtown Ventura is seen here in the 1860s. Mission San Buenaventura's bell tower can be seen down the road on the right. Pres. Abraham Lincoln signed a proclamation on May 23, 1862, that returned the mission's church, clergy residence, cemetery, orchard, and vineyard to the Catholic Church. (Courtesy of San Buenaventura Conservancy.)

When this photograph of Main Street in downtown Ventura was taken on July 4, 1874, the United States had been independent for 98 years and California had been a state for 24 years. (Courtesy of Los Angeles Public Library.)

32

Early pioneers Johannes Borchard (right), first cousin to Edward Borchard, and Albert F. Maulhardt (below) planted sugar beets around the county and found that Oxnard was the prime location to grow the crop. Borchard and Maulhardt invited Henry Thomas Oxnard and his three brothers, owners of the American Beet Sugar factory in Chino, California, to discuss the shipment of beets to the Chino factory and pledged 18,000 acres from local farmers. Henry Oxnard recognized that the sugar beets were superior, and in 1898, he and his three brothers helped finance the construction of a sugar factory in the area once called Rancho Colonia. Five years later, the townsite near the factory became the City of Oxnard. The success of the factory also led to a Southern Pacific Railroad spur line to the plant. (Both, courtesy of California State Library.)

Henry T. Oxnard (1860–1922) was president of the American Beet Sugar Company, later the American Crystal Sugar Company. In 1889, he founded a sugar refinery in Grand Island, Nebraska, and two additional factories in Norfolk, Nebraska, and in Chino, California. The early growth of Oxnard can be attributed to the founding of the Oxnard sugar beet factory, and it is fitting that the city was named after him. Below is a 1918 portrait of the Oxnard brothers. From left to right are James, Robert, Henry, and Benjamin. Henry was also president of the American Beet Sugar Association, which represented all the sugar beet factories in the country, and the brothers controlled all five of their sugar beet factories. (Both, courtesy of Oxnard Public Library.)

Pacific Beet Sugar Company, later American Beet Sugar Factory and then American Crystal Sugar Company, became the largest employer in the area in the 1890s, hiring many Mexican, Chinese, and Japanese laborers. The industry gave impetus to the city's growth and development, making Oxnard the largest city in the county. (Courtesy of Broome Library, CSU Channel Islands.)

Thomas R. Bard (1841–1915) served on the board of supervisors of Santa Barbara County from 1868 to 1873 and was appointed commissioner to organize Ventura County. Bard discussed with railroad and oil baron Thomas Scott the valuable potential of the land and submarine canyon in Oxnard, resulting in the purchase of Rancho El Rio de Santa Clara o la Colonia. The land was subdivided, and the street grid of the town was laid out in 1888. The town became Port Hueneme in 1930 and was incorporated in 1948. (Author's collection.)

35

This is a 1930s aerial view of Port Hueneme, a beach city adjoining Oxnard and the Santa Barbara Channel. Naval Base Port Hueneme was not yet established. Port Hueneme lies within the Oxnard alluvial plain, and the land was used predominately for agriculture. Expansive farmland can be seen surrounding most of the town. (Courtesy of US Navy Seabee Museum.)

Thomas Bard had a wharf constructed in 1872 to help transport the growing agricultural industry's produce. World War II necessitated the taking of Bard's Wharf for a naval base. Six docks were soon constructed that allowed for nine ships, and the surrounding agricultural lands were replaced with buildings, miles of railroad tracks, and other structures. (Courtesy of US Navy Seabee Museum.)

Here is an aerial view of Naval Air Station Point Mugu. Point Mugu is the only large area in the county that is not agricultural. The naval air station operated from 1942 to 2000 and then merged with Naval Construction Battalion Center Port Hueneme as Naval Base Ventura County. It has two runways and includes a 36,000-square-mile sea test range. Below, Pres. John F. Kennedy visits Naval Air Station Point Mugu in 1963. He said, "We did not come here from Washington, DC, to encourage the military forces, but rather to see the military forces encourage ourselves. . . . We have seen for the past 24 hours the military forces of the United States here on the West Coast. I go back to Washington with the feeling of renewed pride in being an American and renewed confidence in being a citizen of the greatest republic on earth." (Both, courtesy of US Navy.)

Adolfo Camarillo (1864–1958), son of Juan and Martina Camarillo, is seen at left. The history of the city of Camarillo began when Juan Camarillo purchased the Mexican land grant Rancho Calleguas from the Ruiz family in 1875. After his death in 1889, his son Adolfo took over operation of the cattle ranch that later included crops, notably lima beans, corn, walnuts, and citrus. Adolfo was popularly known for his horses—Camarillo white horses—that he bred, rode, and showed at parades and events. He also became a prominent figure for his community involvement and leadership roles in the county. Below is Camarillo's Queen Anne Victorian–style home built in 1892. It was listed as a county historic landmark in 1969 and listed in the National Register of Historic Places in 2003. (Both, courtesy of Camarillo Ranch Foundation.)

Seen here is a mid-1930s photograph of citrus orchards and the Camarillo State Hospital at center. The facility was one of the largest psychiatric hospitals in the country at the time and operated from 1930 to 1997. After its closure, the hospital became a branch of California State University and, in 2002, CSU Channel Islands. (Courtesy of Broome Library, CSU Channel Islands.)

Oxnard Air Force Base was in operation from 1940 to 1945 and then again from 1951 to 1970. During World War II, it was primarily a flight training airfield, and during the Cold War, it became part of the Air Defense Command as a fighter-interceptor training base. The base was inactivated in 1970, and the facilities became part of the Camarillo Airport. (Courtesy of California Military History Online.)

This is a 1905 photograph of the Ventura Pier with smoke from a passing ship and a docked ship. Built in 1872, it was once called the San Buenaventura Wharf and later the Ventura Wharf. It served as a commercial wharf to receive lumber and merchandise and to transport agricultural products and oil. The pier was one of the earliest constructed along the coast and was once one of the longest wooden piers in California. (Courtesy of Fillmore Historical Museum.)

The Neoclassical-style building at the far end of the street was once the Ventura County Courthouse, completed in 1912 and used until 1969, when it was declared unsafe in the event of an earthquake. Lawyer and author Erle Stanley Gardner had an office nearby where he wrote the Perry Mason novels. In 1971, the City of Ventura purchased and refurbished the building. In 1974, it was dedicated as Ventura City Hall. The old building is a city, county, and state landmark and is listed in the National Register of Historic Places. (Courtesy of Fillmore Historical Museum.)

The Serra Cross perched on a hill in Ventura overlooking the Santa Barbara Channel is said to have been put there by Father Serra in 1782. It has been replaced three times due to age and windstorms. It is representative of the founding of Mission San Buenaventura and the town of San Buenaventura. (Author photograph.)

Pictured is the Olivas Adobe, registered as California Historical Landmark No. 115 and listed in the National Register of Historic Places. Raymundo Olivas (1809–1879) and his friend Felipe Lorenzana were granted 4,670 acres of Rancho San Miguel. Olivas's house was an impressive two-story hacienda. It was sold many times until "Yeast King" Max Fleischmann purchased and restored it. Upon Fleischmann's death, it was donated to the City of Ventura. (Courtesy of City of Ventura.)

At left is an early photograph of Emilio Carlos Ortega (1857–1942), the 11th child of Emigdio and Maria Conception Jacinta Dominguez Ortega and founder of the Pioneer Green Chili Packing Company in 1898, later the Ortega Chile Packaging Company. Emilio had brought chile seeds from New Mexico and planted them at his family's home in Ventura. When he learned how to preserve and package the chiles, he founded one of the first commercial food operations in the state. Below, the Ortega Adobe was designated Ventura's Historic Landmark No. 2 in 1974. Emigdio Ortega built the original three-room house in 1857, where he and his wife, Maria, raised their 13 children. It was here where Emilio first planted and grew the chiles. (Both, courtesy of City of Ventura.)

Three

THE SANTA CLARA RIVER VALLEY

This is an aerial view of the Santa Clara River Valley. The valley is home to the towns of Fillmore, Santa Paula, and Piru. Surrounded today by predominately citrus and avocado orchards and framed by mountains that rise to over 5,000 feet above sea level, the area is also known as the Heritage Valley. (Photograph by Chevy111, Wikimedia Commons.)

Pictured is an inviting 1961 billboard placed at the east city limits encouraging residency in Fillmore. The cornucopia depicts an abundance of seasonal locally grown fruits. Fillmore is at the foot of the Topatopa Mountains in the Santa Clara Valley, which runs east-west and is approximately four miles wide. Situated at the junction of the Santa Clara River and Sespe Creek, it was incorporated in 1914 and is one of the oldest incorporated towns in Ventura County. At left is an 1800s photograph of Jerome A. Fillmore, general superintendent for the Southern Pacific Railroad, who oversaw the construction of the rail line laid through the town in 1887 and whom the town was named after. (Both, courtesy of Fillmore Historical Museum.)

This is an aerial view of Fillmore nestled between expansive agricultural lands and mountains. The Europeans of the Portolá Expedition were the first to venture inland. They came upon the Santa Clara River Valley and set up camp in the Fillmore area in 1769. (Courtesy of Fillmore Historical Museum.)

Here is an early-1900s photograph of walnut harvesting. Two men with long hooked poles shake walnuts loose from trees while several men, women, and children gather the fallen nuts. Walnut trees commonly grow 50 feet or taller. From the mid-1800s until approximately the 1930s, farmers in the Santa Clara River Valley mostly grew walnuts and engaged in dry farming. Citrus was widely grown in the valley when reliable water sources were discovered and tapped. (Courtesy of Library of Congress.)

Pictured is an early-1900s farm scene of several men, women, and a child after harvested walnuts were packaged in crates and burlap bags. Walnuts were first planted in California in the 1800s. Prior to the 1860s, the valley was primarily used for dry farming of barley, beans, and grains. (Courtesy of Fillmore Historical Museum.)

Fillmore's economy has primarily been agricultural, and most of its industries are related to citrus and avocado orchard farming, packing, and more recently, specimen tree farming. Although there is some row crop farming, the Santa Clara River Valley predominately grows citrus and avocados. (Courtesy of Fillmore Historical Museum.)

The Santa Clara River Valley's towns and agricultural industry blossomed when the railroad came to the valley and opened the door to the outside world. Although Santa Paula was already a major agricultural center by the time the rail line came to the valley in 1887, it further widened the industry's agricultural reach and developed the towns of Fillmore and Piru through successful commerce. (Courtesy of Fillmore Historical Museum.)

In 1852, Wells Fargo & Co. was founded to serve the West. It bought gold, delivered gold and valuables, offered banking services, and transported money. By 1918, it also delivered mail and goods, including agriculture products. Remote farm areas relied on and benefitted from its services, which helped the growth of small towns. (Courtesy of Fillmore Historical Museum.)

This is a 1912 photograph of Fillmore's train depot. Three workers are seen performing maintenance along the tracks using a water hose and tampers to pack and level dirt before maintenance-of-way was mechanized. At center is Franklin Salee, a section foreman for Southern Pacific. (Courtesy of Fillmore Historical Museum.)

In this 1915 photograph, people wait for the train at Fillmore's train depot. The rail line was part of the Southern Pacific's main line between Los Angeles and San Francisco and was extensively used for passenger transport and to haul citrus from packinghouses in the valley until the 1950s. (Courtesy of Fillmore Historical Museum.)

A three-mule team pulls a covered wagon to the Fillmore train depot in the early 1900s. The railroad brought a wealth of ease for farmers and residents of the valley. The ability to send and receive goods via rail, including passenger transport, allowed small farmers to prosper and enabled people to more easily travel to and from the valley. (Courtesy of Fillmore Historical Museum.)

Stacks of orange crates are ready for shipment. The first refrigerated means of transport was on trains. Refrigeration allowed large quantities of perishable produce to be transported from remote farms to urban areas. In the 1950s and 1960s, the development of mechanized equipment expanded the volume of fruits that could be processed, including cold storage facilities to store fruit for long periods. (Courtesy of Fillmore Historical Museum.)

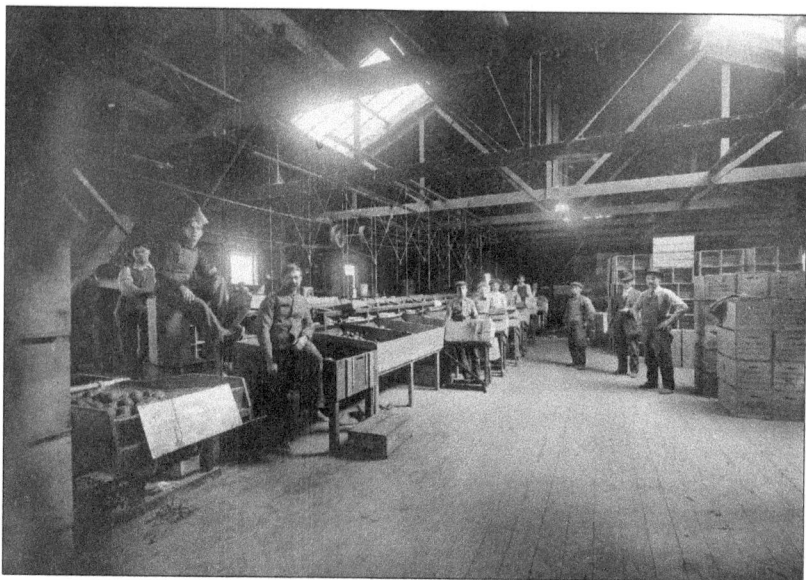

Pictured is the first Fillmore orange packinghouse, built in 1925. Several workers are at their stations, ready to pack fruit. Here, the packinghouse received locally grown oranges to sort according to size and quality and then wash, dry, and pack them into crates. (Courtesy of Fillmore Historical Museum.)

This is a 1909 view of the interior of the Fillmore Citrus Association Packing House. The packinghouse was at 341 A Street. Sunkist Growers later operated out of the packinghouse for several years until the facility was sold and used as a repurposed creative campus. (Courtesy of Fillmore Historical Museum.)

Seen here in 1930, James and Walter Beem are at the Fillmore lemon packinghouse loading crates of Sespe label lemons into a boxcar. Many packinghouses were built in the 1920s and 1930s due to the citrus planting frenzy that began in the late 1800s and the orange industry boom that followed. (Courtesy of Fillmore Historical Museum.)

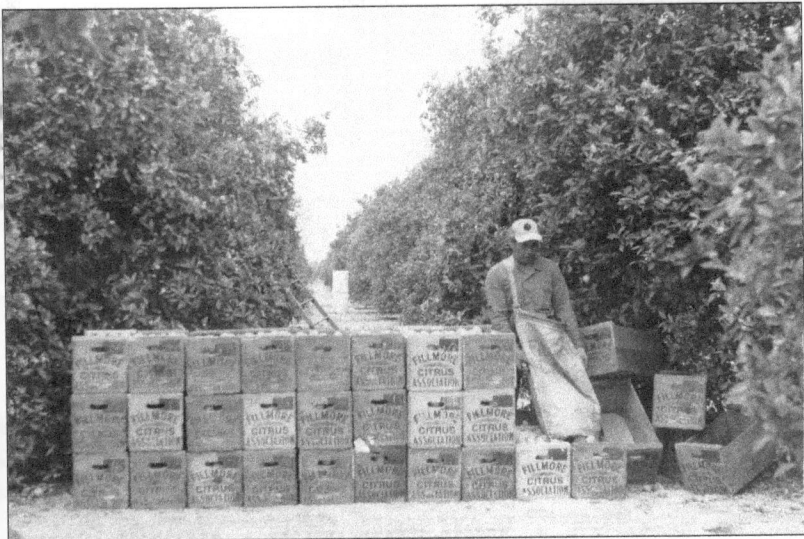

A farm worker fills crates of harvested oranges directly from the orchard for the Fillmore Citrus Association. (Courtesy of Fillmore Historical Museum.)

Small farm growers used family members to help pick oranges, including children. Below, a crew of 12 Japanese workers harvest oranges in Santa Paula. The California orange boom in the early 1900s depended on hired farm labor more than other agricultural states. By 1909, there were 30,000 Japanese farm laborers in the state. They dominated in the fields until Japanese immigration was restricted. In 1917, growers turned to Mexico for their labor needs, and Filipinos were also brought to the United States to meet agricultural labor demand. (Both, courtesy of Fillmore Historical Museum.)

This is an early-1900s photograph of apricot sun-drying in Bardsdale. By the early 1900s, California's commercial dried fruit industry boomed, and there were 290 acres of apricots planted in Bardsdale. Growing apricots in California dates to the founding of Mission San Buenaventura, when Spanish missionaries brought apricots to California. Here, several women, men, and children stand by flats containing thousands of drying apricots. The process was laborious, requiring picking, sorting by size and color, cleaning, and pitting before the fruit could be laid out to sun dry. Below is a photograph of adult workers and children preparing apricots for sun-drying by placing the prepared fruit on wooden flats. In 1904, it was reported that there were 500 pitters working in the apricot orchards near Piru. (Both, courtesy of Fillmore Historical Museum.)

Seen here is an early-1900s photograph of a woman who came to the valley to harvest apricots. In the late 19th and early 20th century, people came from Los Angeles and other cities to work the valley's apricot harvest. People from out of town often stayed in small labor camp houses where cooking and washing were done outside. (Courtesy of Fillmore Historical Museum.)

This is a 1915 photograph of a Santa Paula dairy. Dairying in Ventura County began with the founding of Mission San Buenaventura when the mission ranched large herds of cattle. Settlers who spread around the county also began dairying, and many farmers had their own dairy cow for their family's milk and butter. (Courtesy of Fillmore Historical Museum.)

Saddled ranchers rope cattle in this early-1900s photograph taken on a cattle ranch in the Santa Clara River Valley. The oldest operating cattle ranch in the county is Aliso Ranch. It was purchased from James Willouby in 1910 and became the headquarter ranch of the Hobson Brothers Packing Company. (Courtesy of Fillmore Historical Museum.)

Sheep graze around oil rigs in the hills surrounding Fillmore and Santa Paula. Sheep ranching in the county also began with the founding of Mission San Buenaventura. Livestock ranching was the primary industry during the Spanish and Mexican eras in California. Thomas Bard and Nathan Blanchard, among others who owned livestock, grazed sheep in the county's hills, valleys, and islands. (Courtesy of Fillmore Historical Museum.)

Deeter Turkey Ranch in Fillmore was established in 1938 and raised approximately 20,000 turkeys each year and supplied the county with turkeys for decades. In the 1970s, Exotic Newcastle disease killed all the turkeys at the ranch. The disease also infected the chickens at nearby Julius Goldman's Egg City, which housed over 3,000,000 chickens on 300 acres and produced over 2,000,000 eggs daily. The chickens had to be destroyed. (Courtesy of Fillmore Historical Museum.)

Pictured is an 1882 oil field in Grimes Canyon. The county's many rich oil resources have made Ventura County the "Mother of Oil," with the first production of oil in commercial quantities in the state. Three-fourths of the producing wells in the county are within a six-mile radius of Fillmore. (Courtesy of Fillmore Historical Museum.)

This is an early-1900s photograph of a 10-mule team pulling an oil tank cart uphill to be filled. The three oil barons of the valley were Wallace Hardison, Lyman Stewart, and Thomas R. Bard. When the oil companies combined in 1890, they became Union Oil Company. (Courtesy of Fillmore Historical Museum.)

Seen here is an 1802 view of oil field workers at the Robertson oil lease near Bardsdale. Most oil leases were on rural land in the Santa Paula and Fillmore area. Seated at left is Ross Wileman with his two young sons Ebbie (left) and Donnie. (Courtesy of Fillmore Historical Museum.)

This is a 1915 photograph of living quarters provided for Calumet oil lease workers near the area of Bardsdale. Eight small cottages housed workers and their families. The quarters were located near the oil drilling site. Calumet Oil & Gas had several oil rigs in the Santa Clara River Valley. (Courtesy of Fillmore Historical Museum.)

The Texas Company Fillmore Works is seen here looking northwest in 1931. The image shows the steam still, crude shell stills Nos. 7, 8, and 9, crude pipe still No. 1, and pressure still unit No. 1. The term "still" refers to any form or mixture of gasses that are produced in refineries. (Courtesy of Fillmore Historical Museum.)

This is a mid-1800s photograph of Smith Bros. General Merchandise store in the Santa Clara River Valley. The store sold groceries, hardware, paints and oils, farm machinery, tents, awnings, lumber, hay, grain feed, agricultural implements, iron pipes, and fittings, among other things. Three women are on the balcony, looking out. (Courtesy of Fillmore Historical Museum.)

Bardsdale schoolhouse was built in 1889 at a cost of $1,722. The town of Bardsdale was established in 1887, the same year the Southern Pacific Railroad built a rail line through the valley. The railroad generated growth in the valley in both business and population, necessitating the building of houses, schools, stores, and businesses. (Courtesy of Fillmore Historical Museum.)

Sespe Post Office is pictured in the late 1920s. Although much of the Santa Clara River Valley grew and prospered with the coming of the railroad, Sespe did not develop along with Santa Paula, Fillmore, and Piru as anticipated. The Sespe depot closed after being open for only a few years, and the post office closed in 1932. (Courtesy of Fillmore Historical Museum.)

Central Avenue in downtown Fillmore is seen here in the early 1900s. The small town began to flourish after the railroad came to Fillmore in 1887 and continued to grow until the 1920s. Its classic turn-of-the-20th-century architecture housed Pacific Southwest Bank, a theater, the Masonic Temple, Farmers & Merchants Bank, a drugstore, a grocery store, and many other small businesses. (Courtesy of Fillmore Historical Museum.)

This is a 1922 photograph of the Fillmore Fire Department. Founded in 1914, it was all-volunteer. The firefighters are, from left to right, Cliff Travers, Gus Peres, Cot Mosling, Leon Harthorn, John Strickland, Merl Harthorn, George Mosling, and Ray Lindenfeld. The Fillmore chief of police, Earl Hume, is on the motorcycle. (Courtesy of Fillmore Historical Museum.)

Pictured are a group of young men and boys in a Charlie Chaplin lookalike contest held at the Fillmore Towne Theatre in 1923. The theater was built in 1916 and had a single screen that showed silent films. Its stage was used for vaudeville. (Courtesy of Fillmore Historical Museum.)

Pictured is one of the county's earliest spa resorts at the Sespe hot springs. The resort offered private bathing in the therapeutic waters. The entrepreneur of the resort is seated in front of a makeshift tent. Below is a view of a guest bathing inside an open-air tent. There are many hot springs in the county, one being Matilija Hot Springs, discovered in 1873 by J.W. Wilcox, who thought the waters could be used for medicinal purposes. In 1875, R.M. Brown owned the Matilija Hot Springs property and began building a resort but sold the property to Captain Gardner. Gardner opened the resort to the public in 1877 and later sold the property in 1881 to a Mr. Wilcoxen, who used the resort as a private home. The property changed ownership many times, with a history rich in colorful events that reflect the era of growth in California. (Both, courtesy of Fillmore Historical Museum.)

From left to right above are Thomas R. Bard (1841–1915), Lyman Stewart (1840–1923), and Wallace L. Hardison (1851–1909), oil barons in Ventura County. In 1886, Stewart and Hardison founded a successful oil company called Hardison and Stewart Oil Company. The company rendered 15 percent of all oil production in California. It merged with Thomas Bard's Sespe Oil and Torrey Canyon Oil to form Union Oil Company in 1890. The new company's headquarters was in Santa Paula. Below is the Union Oil Company building at 1003 East Main Street in Santa Paula. The Queen Anne–style building was erected in 1889 and also housed the Santa Paula Hardware store and post office on the ground floor. Union Oil Company occupied the second floor until it moved its headquarters to Los Angeles in 1900 but continued to use the second floor as a field office. (Both, courtesy of Port Hueneme Historical Museum.)

Nathan W. Blanchard Sr. was regarded as one of the founders of Santa Paula. He was the founder of the citrus giant Limoneria in 1893. Santa Paula became one of the leaders in citrus agriculture. With the citrus and oil industries booming, Santa Paula became a city amid citrus orchards. (Courtesy of Santa Paula Historical Society.)

This is an 1887 photograph of David C. Cook, a wealthy publisher of religious tracts and regarded as the founder of Piru. Cook laid out the town of Piru in 1888 and envisioned creating a "second Garden of Eden," planting 900 acres of apricots, dates, figs, grapes, and other nut and fruit trees, which were recorded biblical foods. (Courtesy of Fillmore Historical Museum.)

Cook built a Victorian Queen Anne–style mansion in Piru, known today as the Cook Mansion or Newhall Mansion. It was sold in 1912 and again in 1968. The grand Victorian home was damaged in a 1971 earthquake and destroyed by fire in 1981. The owners rebuilt it from old photographs. (Courtesy of Fillmore Historical Museum.)

This is a view of the Piru area. It was originally a citrus stop town. David Cook laid out the plans for the town in 1887. That same year, a large Methodist-Episcopal church was built, a post office was opened, and a general merchandise store was established. (Courtesy of Fillmore Historical Museum.)

Above is a 1920 photograph of a wagon pulled by two horses taken at the side of the Piru Cooperative building. Three women and a young boy are seen in the wagon and a man is at the buckboard with a woman sitting next to him. Piru area farmers belonged to an agricultural cooperative that allowed farmers to run a farm in cooperation with other farmers to increase profits and gain collective bargaining power with laborers and packers. It also enabled them to own and control business enterprises, such as buying supplies and services and selling their products. At left, a man drives a horse-drawn carriage past a Piru fruit and vegetable market. (Both, courtesy of Fillmore Historical Museum.)

This is a late-1800s photograph of a general merchandise store in Piru, possibly the C.J. French Co. Some stores were part of the Blue & White Stores, owned locally by an independent dealer, but with goods purchased from Blue & White. (Courtesy of Fillmore Historical Museum.)

The Piru depot closed to passengers in 1938 and to freight transport in 1953. When the Southern Pacific Railroad came to the valley, it had plans to build a depot in nearby Camulos, so it bypassed Piru. David Cook decided to build a depot himself in 1888. A cross was placed atop the building after the depot closed, and the building was leased to the San Salvador Catholic Church. (Courtesy of Fillmore Historical Museum.)

Rancho Camulos was part of the 48,612-acre Rancho San Francisco granted to Antonio del Valle in 1839. His son Ygnacio del Vallee established Camulos Ranch in 1853. The ranch's agricultural history has made it a state and national historic landmark. Rancho Camulos grew the first oranges in the county, and its oranges were the first to be commercially shipped in 1876. The ranch also grew grapes and produced wine and brandy. In the 1860s, ninety acres of grapes were planted and a winery was built. Camulos Ranch became one of the largest vintners in the San Buenaventura Township of Santa Barbara County. Below is a 1933 photograph of historic Casa Del Rancho Camulos and its walnut trees. Citrus, apricot, and peach trees were also grown on the ranch, as well as crops of wheat, corn, and barley. (Both, courtesy of Library of Congress.)

Four

THE OJAI AND
SIMI VALLEYS

Pictured is a map
of the Spanish and
Mexican ranchos
of Ventura County
illustrated by the
Title Insurance and
Trust Company
of Ventura. The
17,717-acre Rancho
Ojai lies between
Ranchos Santa Ana
and Cañada Largo
o Verde, and the
113,009-acre Rancho
Simi is surrounded
by Ranchos Sespe,
Las Posas, Calleguas,
and El Conejo.
(Author's collection.)

This is an aerial view of the Ojai Valley, with Lake Casitas in the background. The valley is approximately ten miles long and three miles wide, divided into the lower and upper valleys. The Ventura River flows through the valley from the surrounding mountains to the north and east, emptying into the Pacific Ocean at the city of Ventura. (Photograph by Ken Lund.)

Charles Nordhoff (1830–1901) first visited Ojai in 1881, and in 1882 mentioned the Ojai Valley in the second published edition of his book *California for Health, Pleasure, and Residence: A Book for Travelers and Settlers.* The town of Ojai was originally named after Nordhoff but renamed in 1917 due to anti-German sentiment during World War I. (Courtesy of Ojai Valley Museum.)

This is an 1800s photograph of Robert Ayers, who came
to Ojai in 1868 with his wife and seven children.
The Ayers family was the first American family
to settle in the valley. Ayers purchased a ranch
in Upper Ojai in 1868, and in 1872 purchased
a ranch in Lower Ojai. In 1887, he purchased
Casitas Ranch and raised racehorses that
were considered to be the finest in the
county. (Courtesy of Ojai Valley Museum.)

This is an 1800 photograph of Olive
Mann Isbell (1824–1899), Ojai's first
schoolteacher and said to be the first
teacher in California. A relative by
marriage of Isbell, Ariane Andresis,
quoted her: "My first teaching
in California was commenced in
the month of December 1846 in
a room about fifteen feet square,
with neither light or heat other
than that which came through a
hole in the tile roof." (Courtesy of
Mayo Hays O'Donnell Library.)

Above is an 1870s photograph of several businesses in central Nordhoff prior to the construction of the arcade. While the larger cities were building brick-and-mortar buildings, the simple wood structures in Ojai at the time were typical American West and included a livery stable, harness shop, saloon, and hardware store, to name a few. Below, five men stand in front of a blacksmith shop in the 1870s. (Both, courtesy of Ojai Valley Museum.)

Ojai's St. Thomas Aquinas Church is seen here around 1917 when the landscaping was not yet completed. It was the first Catholic church in Ojai. It was built to replace the first wooden church that was destroyed by fire in 1917. In 1995, it was listed in the National Register of Historic Places. (Courtesy of Ojai Valley Museum.)

Edward Drummond Libbey (1854–1925) was a glass industry magnate in Toledo, Ohio. He is credited with the early development of Ojai through his help in the finance, design, and construction of Spanish Colonial Revival–style architecture for downtown Ojai. (Courtesy of Ojai Valley Museum.)

Edward Libbey's legacy in Ojai was his vision for the city and the 1917 construction of the Spanish-style arcade, bell tower/post office, and pergola. In 1975, the post office tower and sidewalk portico became Ventura County Historical Landmark No. 26. (Courtesy of Ojai Valley Museum.)

Seen here is a 1902 photograph of bathers on the steps of the Plunge at Matilija Hot Springs. The indoor pool was 150 feet long and 65 feet wide. It also had individual dressing rooms, electric lights, and a covered dance pavilion. Buildings had to be replaced at other Matilija Canyon camps through the years as they were damaged or destroyed by floods. (Courtesy of Ojai Valley Museum.)

Star Camp Congress near Meiners Oaks is pictured in 1928. Thousands of members of the Esoteric Section of the Theosophical Society camped in tents to listen to an inspirational speaker. In 1911, the Order of the Star in the East was founded by Annie Besant and C.W. Leadbeater, who helped purchase land in Ojai for the group. It became an international movement, with Star Camps in the Netherlands and in Ojai. (Courtesy of Ojai Valley Museum.)

Sherman Day Thacher, left, and Olympic swimming gold medalist Duke Paoa Kahanamoku of Hawaii are pictured at Thacher School in 1922. In 1889, Thacher founded the Thacher School in Ojai, a private boarding school overlooking the valley. Once a boys school and later co-ed, it is the oldest co-ed boarding school in California. Duke Kahanamoku was invited to the school to give swimming instruction to the students. (Courtesy of Ojai Valley Museum.)

The Libbey Bowl is seen here in the 1950s. Built in the Libbey's Civic Center Park, it was called Civic Center Bowl, Festival Bowl, and other names through the years. It later became known as Libbey Bowl in the 1980s. The bowl hosted many cultural events and musical performances through the years. It added to the peaceful yet lively, colorful, and quaint landscape of Ojai. (Courtesy of Libbey Bowl.)

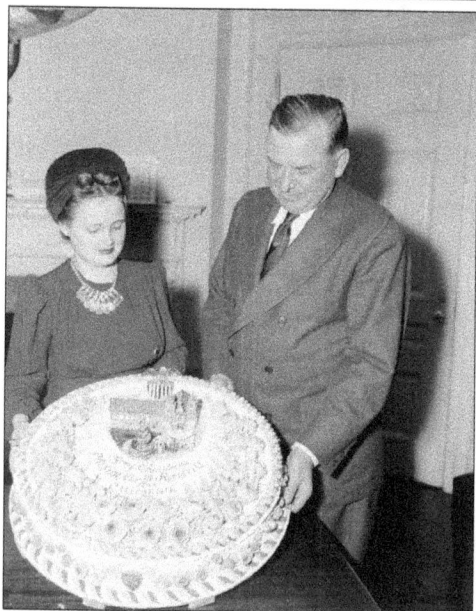

Seen here is a fruitcake baked by W.C. Baker of Ojai. Presidential aide Brig. Gen. Edwin Watson, on the right, accepts the cake from Mildred Cook, secretary to Rep. A.J. Elliott of California, as a gift for Pres. Franklin Roosevelt. Baker had baked cakes for the White House for almost 20 years. (Courtesy of Library of Congress.)

This aerial view of Simi Valley shows it nestled between mountains and hills. Also known as Rancho San José de Nuestra Señora de Altagracia y Simí, Rancho Simi was one of California's largest land grants. Santiago Pico first received the land grant in 1795. After his death in 1815, the rancho was re-granted to his sons Javier, Patricio, and Miguel. (Photograph by Afred Twu.)

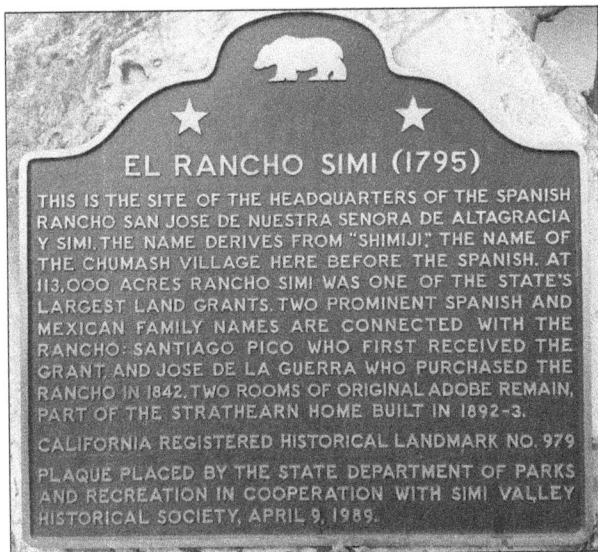

This Rancho Simi plaque is at the Robert P. Strathearn Historical Park in Simi Valley. It commemorates the site of Rancho Simi's headquarters, where two rooms of the original adobe remain part of the Strathearn house, built in 1892. (Author photograph.)

EL RANCHO SIMI (1795)

THIS IS THE SITE OF THE HEADQUARTERS OF THE SPANISH RANCHO SAN JOSE DE NUESTRA SENORA DE ALTAGRACIA Y SIMI. THE NAME DERIVES FROM "SHIMIJI," THE NAME OF THE CHUMASH VILLAGE HERE BEFORE THE SPANISH. AT 113,000 ACRES RANCHO SIMI WAS ONE OF THE STATE'S LARGEST LAND GRANTS. TWO PROMINENT SPANISH AND MEXICAN FAMILY NAMES ARE CONNECTED WITH THE RANCHO: SANTIAGO PICO WHO FIRST RECEIVED THE GRANT, AND JOSE DE LA GUERRA WHO PURCHASED THE RANCHO IN 1842. TWO ROOMS OF ORIGINAL ADOBE REMAIN, PART OF THE STRATHEARN HOME BUILT IN 1892-3.

CALIFORNIA REGISTERED HISTORICAL LANDMARK NO. 979

PLAQUE PLACED BY THE STATE DEPARTMENT OF PARKS AND RECREATION IN COOPERATION WITH SIMI VALLEY HISTORICAL SOCIETY, APRIL 9, 1989.

This is a late-1800s photograph of the Strathearn house. Robert (foreground) and Mary Strathearn (left) purchased approximately 15,000 acres of El Rancho Simi and built their house in front of the Simi adobe. They had seven children. The adobe can be seen connected to the back of the house. They used the adobe rooms as a kitchen and dining room. (Courtesy of Strathearn Historical Park and Museum.)

A six-horse team used for dry-land farming in Simi Valley is seen here in the late 1800s. In 1887, the Simi Land and Water Company was founded. The company sold and leased land in the valley for ranching and farming. Dry farming and livestock ranching soon dominated the valley until the 1950s. (Courtesy of Library of Congress.)

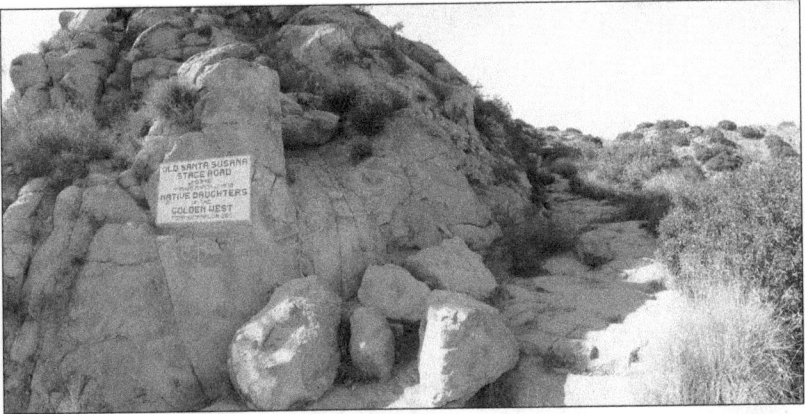

Old Santa Susana Stage Road, also called Santa Susana Pass Wagon Road, was in use from 1859 to 1890 as a stagecoach route. A second road built north of it was a graded dirt road called the New Santa Susana Pass Road and was in use from 1895 to 1917. A third road was built in 1917, north of the second road, and called Santa Susana Pass Road. A portion of the road has been designated as a historic-cultural monument, is listed in the National Register of Historic Places, and was declared a county historical landmark. Below is an 1890 photograph of Joe Horner in a stage wagon on the Old Santa Susana Stage Road. Horner ran the Simi Stage from Simi Hotel to San Fernando. (Above, photograph by Churnice, Wikimedia Commons; below, courtesy of Water and Power Associates.)

This is an aerial view of the Santa Susana Field Laboratory, which sprawls over 2,000 acres in the Simi Hills. The laboratory was established in 1947 and is most known for the development and testing of rocket engines, conducting 17,000 tests in the following 60 years. It supported almost every significant space program in US history. Several agencies and companies occupied the site through the years, including Rocketdyne, Atomics International, and the Boeing Company. Atomics International built and operated the first commercial nuclear power plant in the country. Below is a photograph of rocket engine testing that took place at the site. Each testing area had multiple firing positions. The laboratory provided significant data for the development and improvement of weapons and space vehicles, from the Atlas intercontinental ballistic missile to the space shuttle main engines. The laboratory ceased operation in 2006. (Both, courtesy of Rocketdyne.)

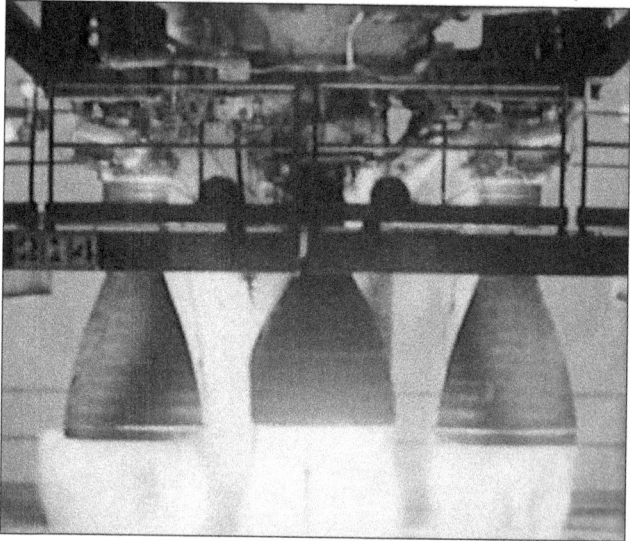

Actor Ray Corrigan (1902–1976) is pictured on horseback above on a late-1940s postcard of the Corriganville amusement park that opened in 1949. The park included a rodeo arena, a small lake with boats, stagecoach rides, and Western-themed entertainment such as live stunts, gunfights, and fistfights in a Western street setting called Silvertown, and was a big attraction in the valley. Corriganville began when Ray Corrigan purchased a 1,500-acre ranch in Simi Valley in 1937, and filming for movies and television shows began on the property, which became known as Corriganville Movie Ranch. Film crews lived in buildings on the property, and it became a small movie industry community. Below is a photograph of a fire truck of the all-volunteer Corriganville Fire Department. In 1966, Bob Hope purchased the ranch, and it was renamed Hopetown. Hopetown was short-lived, closing after a year. (Both, courtesy of Robert C. Pavlik.)

Pictured above are Pres. Ronald Reagan and Nancy Reagan breaking ground for the Ronald Reagan Presidential Library and Museum in Simi Valley on November 21, 1988. The library opened in 1991. The site was chosen by President Reagan because of its picturesque landscape and panoramic views of the valley and ocean. It became the largest of the 13 federally operated presidential libraries in the country. The library is the repository of presidential records from the Reagan administration. It also has become the burial site of both the president and the first lady. Its permanent exhibit covers the life of Reagan. The library holds 50 million pages of presidential documents, over a million photographs, 500,000 feet of motion picture film, and thousands of video and audio tapes. It is the valley's main attraction. Below is a photograph of the entrance to the library. (Both, courtesy of Ronald Reagan Presidential Library.)

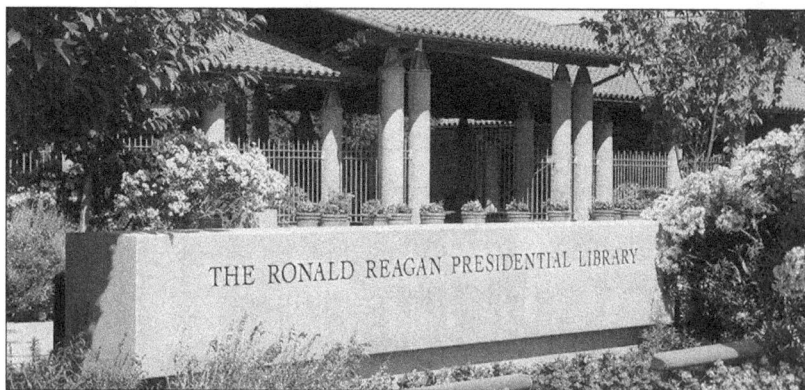

THE RONALD REAGAN PRESIDENTIAL LIBRARY

Five

THE CONEJO VALLEY

This aerial view of the Conejo Valley is from 1972. The valley was a 48,672-acre Spanish land grant given to José Polanco and Ygnacio Rodriguez in 1803. In 1822, the Polanco portion of the land was re-granted to José de la Guerra y Noriega, and later, the Rodriguez portion was granted to Maria del Carmen de Rodriguez. After the Treaty of Guadalupe Hidalgo in 1848, the grants were patented to de la Guerra and Maria del Carmen de Rodriguez in 1873. (Photograph by Frank Knight.)

At left is an 1880 photograph of Howard Mills, one of Conejo Valley's early land developers. Mills and his partner John Edwards purchased 23,835 acres from the de La Guerra heirs. Mills donated two acres of his land to build the first school in the valley. The school was built in 1877 and named Conejo School, pictured below. The building had three paneled windows on each side for light and was white with a red gable roof. The school was built during the year of the drought (1876–1877), which forced many families to leave the valley. Mills went bankrupt and sold his property in 1881 to Andrew Russell and his brother Hannibal. (Both, courtesy of Stagecoach Inn Museum.)

Seen here is an 1870 photograph of Andrew Durkee Russell. He and his brother Hannibal purchased the Triunfo Ranch in 1881 for $15,000 from Howard Mills. The Russell brothers used the land for cattle ranching. Andrew's son Joseph H. Russell became a local cattle rancher and author. (Courtesy of Stagecoach Inn Museum.)

Pictured is an early photograph of John Edwards. In 1893, Edwards sold 10,000 acres of what is now Central Thousand Oaks to Edwin and Harold Janss. Edwin Janss Sr. built a house on the ranch and used it as the ranch's headquarters and a weekend getaway for him and his wife, Florence. (Courtesy of Stagecoach Inn Museum.)

This is a 1967 aerial view of Westlake Village and dam during the early development of the island. Highway 101 can be seen at center. Lindero Canyon is at bottom right, and Triunfo Canyon Road is at left. (Courtesy of Stagecoach Inn Museum.)

This is another aerial view of Westlake Village Island and surrounding neighborhoods. Triunfo Canyon Road winds on the left. A portion of Lindero Canyon Road can be seen at bottom. Approximately two-thirds of the community was annexed by the City of Thousand Oaks. (Courtesy of Stagecoach Inn Museum.)

Egbert Starr Newbury (1843–1880) founded the town of Newbury Park. He was the first newspaper reporter in the valley and established the Newbury Park Post Office in 1875, with he and his wife, Fannie, becoming postmasters. The Newburys left Newbury Park and moved to Michigan due to the drought of 1876–1877. (Courtesy of Stagecoach Inn Museum.)

This is a 1902 photograph of the Newbury Park Post Office sign with a saddled horse tied to the post. Twenty-three-year-old Samuel Sergeant Newbury, the only child of Egbert and Fannie Newbury, traveled to the valley on horseback to visit his family's former home. A passerby took the picture, which Samuel sent to his mother. (Courtesy of Stagecoach Inn Museum.)

Seen here is a family portrait of the Caspar and Theresa Maring Borchard family in 1893. From left to right are (first row) Frank, Charles, and Teresa; (second row) Caspar, Theresa, Caspar Sr., and Antone; (third row) Mary, Rosa, and Leo. From the mid-1800s to 1882, the Borchards purchased more than 8,000 acres and were among the early pioneers in the Conejo Valley. (Courtesy of Stagecoach Inn Museum.)

This is an early photograph of Cecil Haigh, who purchased the Grand Union Hotel and 1,000 acres in Conejo Valley in 1885. His cousin Cicelie Flora Haigh, whom he married in 1892, ran the kitchen at the hotel, and Cecil operated the hotel. In 1888, Cecil sold two acres of his land for a school site. Before the school was built, classes were held at the hotel. Haig's descendants owned the hotel building until 1964, when it was donated to the Conejo Recreation and Park District. (Courtesy of Stagecoach Inn Museum.)

The Timber School and bell tower are seen above in 1889. The white wooden schoolhouse with green trim was named after the community of Timberville. Miss Mosher was the first teacher. The school had one room with two small anterooms for boys' and girls' cloakrooms, with the two entrance doors leading into the cloakrooms. Two outhouses were behind the building. The schoolhouse was also used for church services and community activities. Below are students and teacher E.S. McGrew, center, in 1898. In 1924, a new two-room schoolhouse with running water and electricity was built in front of the original school, which was demolished in 1925, and an auditorium was constructed in 1948. The school and auditorium buildings are City of Thousand Oaks historical landmarks. (Both, courtesy of Stagecoach Inn Museum.)

A stagecoach with a team of six horses is in front of the Stagecoach Inn in the 1930s. On the coach is an advertisement for Harold's Club in Reno, Nevada. The inn was originally the Grand Union Hotel, built in 1876. From 1887 to 1901, it served as a depot for the Coast Stage Line. (Courtesy of Stagecoach Inn Museum.)

This is an early-1900s blank postcard with a picture of two guests on horseback and a young girl riding a donkey at the Stagecoach Inn, formerly the Conejo Hotel and originally the Grand Union Hotel. The photograph was taken at the rear of the inn. The guests could have been traveling by horseback and stayed at the inn. (Courtesy of Stagecoach Inn Museum.)

Louis Goebel stands next to Leo the lion. Goebel founded Jungleland USA in 1926 as a support facility for the Hollywood movie industry. Goebel worked at Universal Studios when it closed its animal facility. Five lions from the studio made up Goebel's first collection of wild animals at Jungleland. (Courtesy of Stagecoach Inn Museum.)

Jungleland USA was a private zoo, animal training facility, and animal theme park in Thousand Oaks. The facility was originally called Goebel's Lion Farm, then Goebel's Wild Animal Farm, before it became Jungleland USA. Goebel acquired and trained a variety of exotic animals that he rented to the studios for use in films. (Courtesy of Stagecoach Inn Museum.)

In 1929, the facility opened to the public as a theme park, which became a popular attraction in the 1940s and 1950s. The park featured animal shows and had a female lion tamer. Many television and movie productions used Goebel's animals through the years. The lion mascot of Metro-Goldwyn-Mayer studio was from Jungleland USA. (Courtesy of Stagecoach Inn Museum.)

Jungleland USA also featured trapeze shows. The park closed in 1969, and its animals, buildings, trucks, furniture, and supplies were sold at auction. Although Goebel retained ownership of the land, it was later sold to the city of Thousand Oaks, and is where the Civic Arts Plaza was built. (Courtesy of Stagecoach Inn Museum.)

Six

DISASTERS

On March 14, 1928, the *San Francisco Chronicle* reported on the St. Francis Dam disaster of March 12. It was the worst disaster recorded in Southern California at the time. Lives, homes, structures, crops, and roads were destroyed. The Santa Clara River Valley suffered extreme devastation from the flood. (Courtesy of *San Francisco Chronicle*.)

Pictured is the center section of the dam, which came to be called the "tombstone." To the right, the dam's wing can be seen. The dam collapsed without warning. The tombstone and wing are all that remained. (Courtesy of Fillmore Historical Museum.)

Seen here is a ravished structure near Piru at Torrey Crossing. The path of destruction was 54 miles from the dam site in Los Angeles County down to the Santa Clara River Valley through Ventura and out to the Pacific Ocean. It took approximately five and a half hours for all the water to spill out into the ocean. (Courtesy of Fillmore Historical Museum.)

Uprooted trees and debris are seen along the Santa Clara River bank after the St. Francis Dam collapse. It was almost an hour before the first warning of imminent danger was given to the telephone operator in Ventura, who, after receiving the information, called the local telephone operators and sheriff offices in Fillmore and Santa Paula. When Fillmore chief Earl Hume got the call, he set out to warn residents who lived close to the river, but by the time he could reach the east limits of Fillmore, the flood had hit with a 40-foot wave. Below, Fillmore residents gather on a section of the remaining road amid the debris. (Both, courtesy of Fillmore Historical Museum.)

The flood from the St. Francis Dam collapse devastated the Shiells Walnut Orchard on Guiberson Road. The morning after the flood, the search for survivors began. Neighboring Santa Paula was flooded and suffered much of the same destruction and damage as Fillmore. (Courtesy of Fillmore Historical Museum.)

This image was captured on Highway 23 in Fillmore on the road to Moorpark. Cleanup of uprooted trees, vegetation, and debris took weeks and hundreds of workers. Steam shovels were used to remove trees and wood from houses and structures. Mules, horses, and tractors were also used in the effort. (Courtesy of Fillmore Historical Museum.)

Pictured is the Santa Clara River Bridge that was destroyed in a 1914 flood. The St. Francis Dam disaster was one of many floods that devastated the valley. Recorded floods from storms include the years 1862, 1867, 1884, 1911, 1914, 1938, 1941, 1943, 1944, 1945, 1969, 1978, 1980, 1983, 1992, 1995, 1998, and 2005. (Courtesy of Fillmore Historical Museum.)

The Santa Clara River Bridge was again destroyed in the flood of 1938. Two men seated back-to-back are in a two-passenger cable seat that was rigged for people to cross the river. (Courtesy of Fillmore Historical Museum.)

Three people cross a footbridge that was rigged without a permit for people to cross the Santa Clara River after the bridge was destroyed in the flood of 1938. Although it was dangerous, people who lived across the river had no other way to cross it. Below is a warning sign relieving the Division of Highways of liability for those risking the walk across the footbridge. (Both, courtesy of Fillmore Historical Museum.)

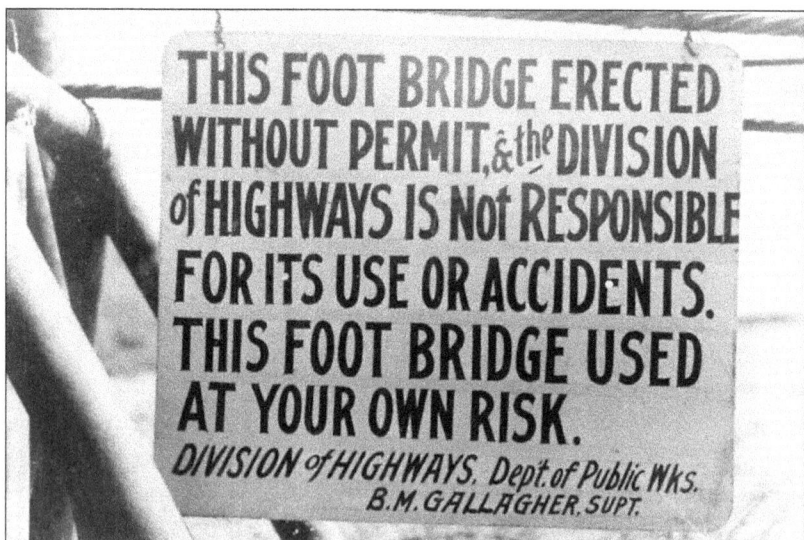

THIS FOOT BRIDGE ERECTED WITHOUT PERMIT, & the DIVISION of HIGHWAYS IS Not RESPONSIBLE FOR ITS USE OR ACCIDENTS. THIS FOOT BRIDGE USED AT YOUR OWN RISK.
DIVISION of HIGHWAYS, Dept. of Public Wks.
B.M. GALLAGHER, SUPT.

Drought was every rancher and farmer's nightmare. Several cattle are seen above at a dry water pond. California's seven-year drought (1928–1934) was a major disaster that became the impetus for reservoir planning and development. The duration of the drought and severity of runoff destroyed the livelihood of many farmers in the state. Below is a rancher driving cattle to be watered and fed in confinement. Confinement feeding helped maintain the health of the livestock, and also helped preserve ground cover and land condition. The drought of 1863 killed massive numbers of livestock all over California. Lack of pasture and water caused thousands of cattle to die of starvation. In Santa Barbara County, an article in the *Daily Alta California* in 1864 stated that 18,000 cattle "have been slaughtered for their hides and tallow, and from one-third to one-half of the remainder have died by starvation." (Both, courtesy of Library of Congress.)

Grazing cattle are brought in for confinement feeding in 1935. Two men guide cattle into a small confined area where they are fed and watered. During a drought, low soil moisture affects plant growth, resulting in reduced forage. Grazing under drought conditions worsens drought effects on both the cattle and the land. Pastures and native ranges become dormant under drought conditions and may be low in vitamin A, phosphorus, and protein, as well as making plants toxic. (Both, courtesy of Library of Congress.)

Above, confined cattle are fed, watered, and inspected in 1935. Drought-affected pastures and native ranges typically do not produce adequate forage for grazing. Many ranchers had to cull their stock, eliminating excess stock that is considered inferior, such as cows that are no longer productive or are determined to not have value. The reduction of the stock benefitted the rancher and the land. As seen below, cattle without adequate food, water, and shelter succumbed to the drought conditions. (Both, courtesy of Library of Congress.)

Pictured above is an abandoned farmhouse during California's drought in 1871. Below is an abandoned farmhouse and barn. A report of the agricultural commissioner for 1874 gave an account of the 1871 drought: "In November 1863, there was a regular downpour, and it did not rain again until November 1864; and in consequence, dead cattle covered the ground from Monterey to Southern California. The year 1877 was very dry. I have heard men say, with a sigh, 'It was the dry year of '77 that broke me up. My sheep all died.' Many a man grew gray that year, as he saw his living withering away. During the three years from 1868 to 1871, south of Monterey neither grass nor grain grew. . . . Hundreds of farms were abandoned, and the stock-men were compelled to drive their cattle, horses, and sheep to the gulches of the mountains, not only for food, but for water." (Both, courtesy of Library of Congress.)

Pictured is a California wheat field devastated by drought in 1897. Wheat is sensitive to drought during the vegetative phase, and drought limits the development of its root system, resulting in decreased leaf area, leaf number per plant, leaf size, and leaf longevity. Frederick Hastings Rindge, the owner of neighboring Rancho Topanga Malibu Sequit in Los Angeles County, said, "Word came from Ventura today that a man up the valley had shot all his range horses rather than see them die, for he could not sell them. Another rancher, with a flock of seven thousand sheep, has found it necessary to kill two thousand young lambs, in order to save the lives of the mother sheep. Some cannot pay their interest, and the mortgage is foreclosed." Below, farmers who lost their livestock, crops, and farms had no choice but to pack up and leave. (Both, courtesy of Library of Congress.)

Newspaper headlines reported that "No city in Ventura County was more devastated by the January 17, 1994 Northridge earthquake than Fillmore." The worst of the city's estimated $250 million in damage was on Central Avenue, the heart of Fillmore's downtown business district. Recorded earthquakes affecting the region that became Ventura County date to 1812. The county has experienced several earthquakes through the years, with damage ranging from light to severe, as was the case in the Northridge earthquake. Below, a mountain of brick, glass, wood, and debris from structures built around the turn of the 20th century fills the downtown sidewalks and street. (Both, courtesy of Fillmore Historical Museum.)

The photograph above shows the extensive earthquake damage to the historic two-story Masonic building in Fillmore. The main street through downtown Fillmore was closed due to rubble and debris and structural uncertainty of the damaged buildings. Below, a Fillmore resident clears his property of debris. Approximately 60 homes and other buildings in Fillmore were damaged by the earthquake. Some were so severely damaged and beyond repair they had to be demolished. Ventura County suffered damage in several other towns and cities. Hundreds of homes, businesses, schools, and a police station in Simi Valley suffered earthquake damage. (Both, courtesy of Fillmore Historical Museum.)

A 1961 fast-burning wildfire threatened the communities of the Santa Clara River Valley. The valley is one of the most dangerous wind and fire corridors in Southern California because of its location between the high desert and the coast, serving as a wind tunnel that funnels high winds and spreads wildfires. (Courtesy of Fillmore Historical Museum.)

The Easy fire in 2019 threatened the Ronald Reagan Presidential Library in Simi Valley. Many large wildfires, including the Woolsey and Thomas fires, have occurred in Ventura County since the early 1900s. The county's rugged terrain, hot and dry weather, seasonal winds, and urban development in the wildlands make the county prone to wildfires. (Photograph by KTLA-TV AP.)

Constructed in 1934, Highway 126 follows the Santa Clara River for 40.55 miles, originating at US Highway 101 in Ventura and ending at Interstate 5 in Santa Clarita. It was a two-lane highway with curvy turns until a four-lane highway was completed in 1998. Pictured here is Highway 126 prior to the completion of four lanes. A 1996 *Los Angeles Times* article on Highway 126 reported 54 fatalities between 1990 and 1994. Prior to becoming a four-lane highway, it was an ominous and dangerous road known as Blood Alley. (Courtesy of Fillmore Historical Museum.)

A large boulder has rolled onto State Route 150 between Santa Paula and Ojai. The bolder was dislodged after a series of storms. The California Department of Transportation used dynamite to break up the bolder and move it off the road. Landslides are common in the county's hills and coastal areas. (Courtesy of California Department of Transportation.)

This is an aerial view of the La Conchita landslide in 2005. The volume of the slide was reported as approximately 200,000 cubic meters with a surface 350 meters long and 80–100 meters wide. The slide killed 10 people, destroyed 13 homes, and damaged over 20 other homes and structures. (Photograph by Doc Searls.)

Seven

A GLIMPSE OF VENTURA COUNTY TODAY

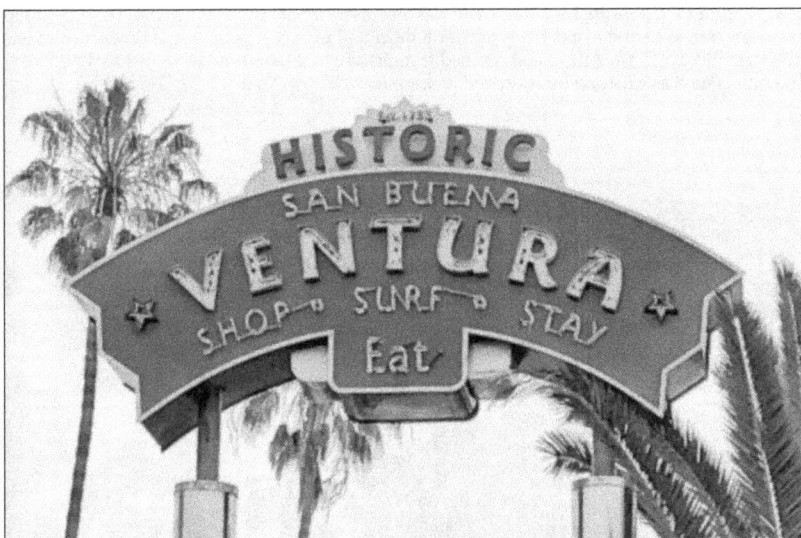

The city of Ventura grew around Mission San Buenaventura. The Ventura Pier became a bustling site with passengers and supplies being transported to and from the city. The pier is still a popular gathering site for fishermen, locals, and tourists. Downtown Ventura is packed with eateries, novelty stores, and many historical sites. Ventura Harbor Village is a working harbor, bringing in fresh seafood daily. Its many restaurants, stores, water activities, and views make the harbor and its village a popular place for locals and tourists. Although much growth has occurred since the mission's founding in 1792, the history of Ventura and Ventura County can still be seen in its architecture, street names, town names, and prominent landmarks that dot the county's cities and towns. (Photograph by Sue and Clay Fischer.)

The Ventura Pier, built in 1872, was once was a transportation and commercial wharf used for passenger transport and as a delivery site for lumber and to export agricultural products and oil. Renovated in 2000, the pier was shortened from its original length of 1,958 feet to 1,600 feet. Today, it is used as a fishing location and pedestrian walkway. (Courtesy of Tony Webster.)

Thousands of people enjoy the sun and sea at Ventura Pier Beach, the most visited beach in the county. The Ventura Pier can be seen in the background. There are over 20 beaches in Ventura County, some of which are state parks. (Courtesy of Allen J. Schaben.)

Pictured is the Ventura Harbor today. The history of the harbor dates to April 8, 1952, when the Ventura Port District was established. The Ventura County Board of Supervisors had ordered the formation of a district. The district was organized for the purpose of constructing and operating a commercial and recreational boat harbor in the city that offered water sport activities, whale watching, harbor cruises, entertainment, and exhibits. The deep-water harbor is still a working harbor. At right, the lighthouse-looking structure is the entrance to the village. The village has many stores, waterfront restaurants, and outdoor courtyards, including an outdoor lawn-amphitheater. (Both photographs by Steven Dale Walker.)

The 10-foot Fishermen's Memorial was created by ceramist Michel Petersen, also known as Michellino, between 2001 and 2005. The memorial site is on the boardwalk close to the harbor's unloading dock by the quay and is in memory of fishermen who lost their lives. Four life-size fishermen are featured on both sides of the memorial. Below, a sailboat cruises by, as seen through the memorial arch. (Both photographs by Steven Dale Walker.)

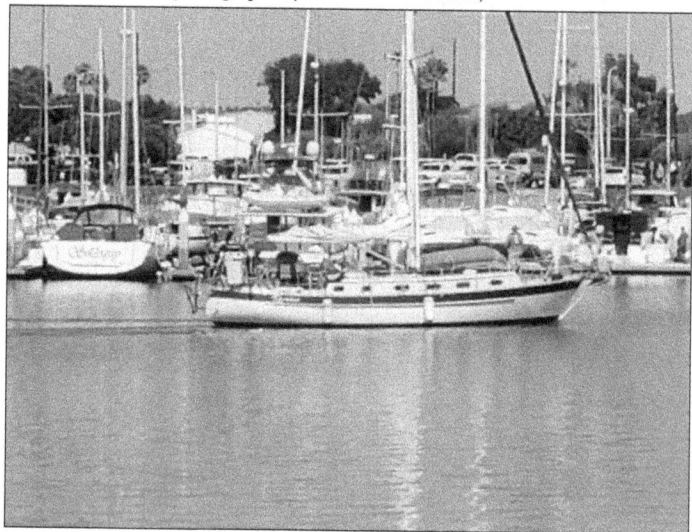

The Channel Islands Harbor is between Port Hueneme and Ventura. The harbor was built in the 1960s by the US Army Corps of Engineers and is the fifth largest harbor in the state for small-boat recreation. Silverstrand Beach is a popular surfing spot, and the harbor was also once a popular Hollywood celebrity spot in the 1920s, hence the name Hollywood Beach. In 1926, Rudolph Valentino filmed a scene for *The Sheik* by an artesian well that is now Lakeshore Drive. Metro-Goldwyn-Mayer Studios and other studios began filming in the area until sound stages were built on studio lots. Below, tsunami hazard zone signs can be seen around surrounding neighborhoods. The last tsunami to hit southern California was on March 11, 2011. Tsunamis are a series of waves typically generated by an earthquake beneath the seafloor. These signs are a warning to seek high ground during an earthquake. (Both photographs by Steven Dale Walker.)

Seen here is a shoreside section of Fisherman's Wharf at Channel Islands Harbor. Once a vibrant and bustling spot with novelty and specialty stores and a place to find fresh seafood, dine at restaurants with harbor views, and enjoy outdoor music entertainment, the wharf fell victim to much-needed revitalization. Disputes exist between Ventura County's harbor department to develop the area with residential units and the City of Oxnard's decision to not allow a zoning change. Below is a portion of the Channel Islands Harbor. Recreational boating, harbor cruises, and water-sport activities keep the harbor busy. (Both photographs by Steven Dale Walker.)

California Street in historic downtown Ventura is seen here. The street is lined with historic buildings that house shops, restaurants, and other businesses. Ventura City Hall, which was once the Ventura County Courthouse, can be seen at the far end of the street. (Courtesy of Fillmore Historical Museum.)

This is an elevated view of the Collection at Riverpark in Ventura. The Collection opened in 2012 as an outdoor lifestyle center with a variety of businesses, including grocery and retail stores, theaters, restaurants, and many other national and regional businesses. (Photograph by Brandon Michaels Group.)

The American flag proudly waves at the memorial for Civil Engineer Corps officers and Seabees who lost their lives during World War II. The memorial is at Naval Base Ventura County Port Hueneme. Below, the iconic Seabee stands guard at the entrance to the World War II memorial. The insignia was created in 1942 and symbolizes an industrious busy bee wearing a Navy hat and equipped with tools and a machine gun, symbolizing that Seabees are ready to fight and defend what they build, hence the Seabee mottos "We Build, We Fight," and "Can Do." (Both photographs by Steven Dale Walker.)

Pictured is an F-4 Phantom II at Point Mugu Missile Park. Below are displays of various missiles and aircraft that were tested at Point Mugu since World War II, including an AMRAAM missile, Regulus submarine-launched missile, Sidewinder missile, Loon missile (an American copy of the German V-1), the BQM-34S "Firebee" aerial target, Polaris ballistic missile, Petrel torpedo, Harpoon missile, Phoenix air-to-air missile, and Bullpup air-to-surface missile. Another aircraft displayed is the F-14 Tomcat. (Both photographs by Steven Dale Walker.)

Above is a 1991 photograph of presidents and first ladies taken in the replica of the Oval Office during the dedication of the Ronald Reagan Presidential Library in Simi Valley. From left to right are Lady Bird Johnson, Jimmy and Rosalynn Carter, Gerald and Betty Ford, Richard and Pat Nixon, Ronald and Nancy Reagan, and George H.W. and Barbara Bush. Below is Air Force One, the plane that flew President Reagan over 660,000 miles to 46 US states and 26 foreign countries during his presidency. (Above, photograph by David Valdez; below, courtesy of Ronald Reagan Presidential Library.)

Seen here is the Pres. Ronald Reagan memorial site at the Reagan Library. The president was laid to rest at the library on June 11, 2004. The inscription reads, "I know in my heart that man is good, that what is right will always eventually triumph and there is purpose and worth to each and every life." Below, the Nancy Reagan memorial site is next to President Reagan's. The first lady was laid to rest on March 11, 2016. (Both, courtesy of Ronald Reagan Presidential Library.)

Seen here is Grandma Prisbrey's Bottle Village in Simi Valley. Tressa Prisbrey (1896–1988) began constructing a village of buildings, walkways, shrines, and sculptures from discarded trash that she collected from the local landfill. The walls seen here are made from thousands of glass bottles. Prisbrey built 16 buildings and structures from glass and other items. The walkway below was made from an assortment of tile pieces. Although the Northridge earthquake of 1994 severely damaged the village, ongoing efforts continue to preserve it. It is designated as a historical landmark by the City of Simi Valley, California Historical Landmark No. 939, and in 1996, was listed in the National Register of Historic Places. (Both, courtesy of Library of Congress.)

The Santa Susana (sometimes spelled Susanna, as seen here) train depot was built in 1903 east of Tapo Street on Los Angeles Avenue. It became a bustling site with telegraph and long-distance passenger and agricultural transport services until its closure in 1974. In 1975, the depot was moved to its present location, adjacent to the Southern Pacific Railroad's main route between San Francisco and Los Angeles, and in 2000 became the Santa Susana Depot and Museum. Below is a 1929 Chevrolet one-ton truck with a Southern Pacific "Daylight" baggage cart, one of the museum's exterior exhibits. (Both photographs by Steven Dale Walker.)

The Santa Paula Depot, built in 1887, was the first train depot in Ventura County. Passenger service ended in 1934, and freight services ended in 1975. Its tracks are used by the Fillmore & Western Railway for tours of the Santa Clara River Valley. In 1972, it was designated a Ventura County historic landmark. (Photograph by Steven Dale Walker.)

Pictured is the Santa Paula Hardware Company building, more commonly known as the Union Oil Company building because Union Oil was founded on the second floor, where the company had its headquarters. The hardware store and post office occupied the ground floor. In 1977, the Ventura County Cultural Heritage Board designated the building a county landmark, and it is also listed in the National Register of Historic Places. (Photograph by Steven Dale Walker.)

This Fillmore city limit sign shows a population of 14,100 as of the 2010 US Census. One of Ventura County's small towns, it has historically been and continues to be predominately an agricultural community. Its historic downtown is quaint, and although businesses come and go, the downtown area still echoes days of old. Below, the rail route through Fillmore, built in 1887, enabled farmers to easily transport their products and also allowed for passenger transport. Passenger travel ended in 1935, and freight transport ended several years later. Today, the Fillmore & Western Railway operates on track owned by the Ventura County Transportation Commission. It offers train tours of the Santa Clara River Valley. (Right, author photograph; below, courtesy of Fillmore Historical Museum.)

The Piru depot closed to passenger transport in 1938 and freight transport in 1953. It was left abandoned until the early 1960s, when a local church used the building as a temporary place of worship. In 1994, the Northridge earthquake severely damaged the structure. In the early 2000s, the Ventura County Redevelopment Project built a new depot at the same location resembling the original depot. Below, Lake Piru is a tributary of the Santa Clara River created in 1955 when the Santa Felicia Dam on Piru Creek was built. (Both photographs by Steven Dale Walker.)

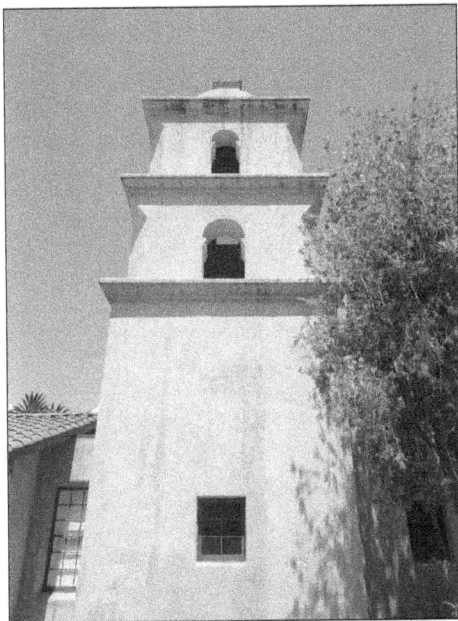

The Ojai Post Office tower was built by Richard S. Requa (1881–1941), a San Diego architect. Edward Libbey envisioned transforming Nordhoff into a beautiful city. Libbey's ideas and Requa's architectural talents produced a magnificent tower for the small town of Nordhoff, later named Ojai. The tower was built in 1916 and is an Ojai landmark. Below, the Ojai Arcade was built in 1917 to give the business district an esthetically appealing look. The arcade was renovated in 1989 by the City of Ojai to preserve the beauty and history of the town. (Both photographs by Steven Dale Walker.)

The pergola in Ojai was spearheaded by David Mason and dedicated on July 4, 1999. It was built in keeping with the spirit of beautification that E.D. Libbey brought to Ojai. There were once arches that led into Civic Park and a pergola covered in wisteria. The arches were demolished in the late 1960s, but the rebuilt pergola continues to be covered in wisteria, and the park was renamed Libbey Park. Below is the Libbey Park fountain. A lion's head fountain once stood in front of the arches that were demolished, serving as a horse trough. The renovation of Libbey Park placed a fountain further back from the entrance. (Both photographs by Steven Dale Walker.)

Pictured is the Sespe Condor Sanctuary in the Topatopa Mountains in the Sespe Wilderness within the Los Padres National Forest north of Fillmore. The sanctuary was established by the US Forest Service in 1947 for the protection of the California condor, the largest bird in North America and an endangered species. The sanctuary comprises 53,000 acres. Below is a California condor in flight. The condor can weigh over 20 pounds, and its wingspan can reach nine feet. Its lifespan in the wild can reach 60 years. (Above, photograph by Ken Lund; below, photograph by Daniel Bianchetta.)

DISCOVER THOUSANDS OF LOCAL HISTORY BOOKS FEATURING MILLIONS OF VINTAGE IMAGES

Arcadia Publishing, the leading local history publisher in the United States, is committed to making history accessible and meaningful through publishing books that celebrate and preserve the heritage of America's people and places.

Find more books like this at
www.arcadiapublishing.com

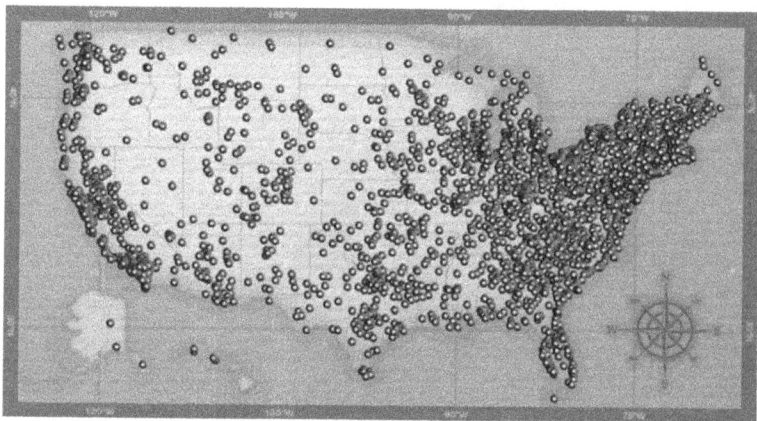

Search for your hometown history, your old stomping grounds, and even your favorite sports team.

Consistent with our mission to preserve history on a local level, this book was printed in South Carolina on American-made paper and manufactured entirely in the United States. Products carrying the accredited Forest Stewardship Council (FSC) label are printed on 100 percent FSC-certified paper.

MADE IN THE USA